CROSSING
BORDERS

autrement dit,
Poèmes Sans Frontières (P.S.F.)

Hilary Rouse-Amadi

Crossing Borders

Published by The Conrad Press in the United Kingdom 2018

Tel: +44(0)1227 472 874
www.theconradpress.com
info@theconradpress.com

ISBN 978-1-911546-32-0

Typesetting and Cover Design by:
Charlotte Mouncey, www.bookstyle.co.uk

The Conrad Press logo was designed by Maria Priestley.

Printed and bound in Great Britain by Clays Ltd, Elcograf S.p.A.

For my sons, my sister and
All the women and men who believe
A better world is possible
And labour, with love, to usher it in.

Special thanks go to Barbara Požgajčić
for her technical assistance,
unfailing support and instinctive
understanding of the worldview
expressed in these poems
and to the always "here to help" staff
of Canterbury Library, whose commitment
to public service shines bright, in our
clouded, profit-over-people, privatising times.

Contents

INTRODUCTION

I think I was born to cross borders, perhaps even before birth that pre-natal essence already the expression of a border crossing, for my Mother was a proud Lancastrian, my Father a Lowland Scot, with an understated, abiding love for his native land.

As a child, I became aware of belonging to at least two cultures, simultaneously distinct yet similar and intertwined. But, I also became aware of painful mysterious tensions, arising from a history of contested encounters and narratives. It was my Mother who told me, when I was still a wean[1], of the hurt she had felt, as a new wife, left wondering why she would never meet the much admired teacher her husband had suggested they visit, sometime after their wedding in nineteen forty five.

After congratulating his former pupil on his recent marriage, with the quip "about time Jim!," Jim's former teacher expressed the hope that he would soon meet the bride, casually asking "and which part of Scotland does the lass come from?" My Father's answer elicited a short awkward silence, followed by a clumsy withdrawal of the invitation warmly extended moments earlier. "Well glancing at my diary, it seems I'm awfully busy for the next few days. Let me have your phone number and I'll see what can be arranged." There was no phone call. Nothing was arranged. My Mother smarted from the sting of rejection and my Father never spoke to his fallen hero again.

Fast forward thirty five years and I recall a lengthy conversation with an Ikwerre friend on the schisms and divisions in Nigerian society, the disruptive histories of slavery, colonial interventions and incursions, the imposition of imperial divisions, the rupture and forced amalgamation of cultures and peoples, followed by flag independence, civil war and neo-colonial exploitation in the era of the so-called oil boom, popularly and more appropriately designated "oil doom." "After all," my friend reminded me, "when you ask why from time to time tensions arise and occasionally erupt between, for example, Yoruba, Igbo and Hausa, I would ask, in return, what of the tensions in your country between Scots, English, Welsh and Irish, furthermore your history of nationhood is considerably longer than that of the state construct known as Project Nigeria."

The poems in this collection move across a multiplicity of borders, visiting some of the problems and challenges of Our Troubled Times. Many celebrate what we share in common, as members of the same species: the human family. Today, more than ever, our children cross borders, exploring and expressing their evolving multiple identities. Is this not to be preferred to the dangers of inward-looking narrow nationalisms and imperial agendas? And so I lay claim to multiple identities, along with Andrey Kurkov, the anonymous World War One veteran, Dr David Nott, Chelsea Manning, Muhammad Ali, Shaker Aamer, Joy Hurcombe, the Igbo heroines of the 1929 Women's War, Celia the Philippine nurse, Irene the Glaswegian granny, the courageous Northern Nigerian women, unlocking doors to new eductional opportunities for their sisters and daughters, the Syrian refugee children......and the many other inspiring voices, honoured in the following pages, where critique, anger, lamentation, hope and celebration abound, for as Alexander Sergeyevich Pushkin (1799-1837), Bertolt Brecht (1898-1956), and Wystan Hugh Auden (1907-1973) have variously insisted, the politics of dark times demand poetic response, a certain kind of music, a certain kind of singing, a certain kind of empathetic and engaging reflection, prefacing the call to action and change.

MOTTO

In the dark times
Will there also be singing?
Yes, there will also be singing
About the dark times.

Bertolt Brecht (1938)

SEE – <u>Bertolt Brecht Poems, Part Two</u> 1929-1938. John Willett and Ralph Manheim editors, with the co-operation of Erich Friel. London: Eyre Methuen, 1976, p.320.

<u>NOTE</u> – wean[1.]- a young child, Lowland Scots.

IDENTITIES IN CRISIS

10th February 2015

Can a Scot, not also be a Briton,
A Briton also a European
And a European, a global citizen,
Just as a multiplicity of sounds
And instruments create a symphony,
A fusion of intertwining identities
True to democratic principles,
A combination of colours and contours,
Weaving enriching harmonies
For every listener and musician?
But, if being a global citizen means
Enslavement to corporate exploitation,
If the direction of European Union
Promotes, all too often, jealous division,
Selfish club members remote from the People,
We will flounder, stranded, in a barren landscape;
And should our Scot become anxious to jump off
A discredited Westminster Ship of State
Piloted, perilous, towards ruinous rocks,
By self-regarding, Little England Boys
Quarrelling, fitful, among themselves,
Separation storms WILL exact a cost,
Fragmentation, a bitter, protracted divorce,

A narrowing of commitments and horizons,
New borders and tariffs subverting the Common Good,
As the democratic impulse is, once more,
Stifled and strangled, struck at the root.

So the question remains, stark, still unanswered:
Why can we not strive harder with honour,
To serve and protect our sisters and brothers,
For a shared planet is to our advantage,
A sine qua non[1] for human survival,
In a time when death cults and barbarous clashes
Run riot, across grim countries and continents?
Nor can we retreat into walled isolation,
In an age of global inter-dependence.
With today's myriad crises in mind:
Blinkered nationalism with hateful eyes,
Empire rebuilding in populist guise
And crazed, theocratic despotism
Consuming nameless, innocent lives,
Identities smashed, justice denied,
The need is urgent, will not be ignored
To end this legacy of hurt and distress,
Crippling a wounded, traumatised world.

So let us revisit this poem's beginning:
Surely a Scot can also be a Briton,

A Briton, also a European

And a European, a world citizen,

When identities find renewal

In a culture of co-operation,

Not the crass, cut-throat competition

Of nihilistic disintegration;

And isn't the time long overdue

To fashion a new Westminster Home,

Where the Common People are welcomed on board,

As democracy calmly rolls up her sleeves

To evict those parasitic, patrician thieves

Serving the interests of the world's super-rich?

And as for me, I am Scottish and English

With links to the Welsh and the Irish;

I am an exasperated European,

A frustrated lover of troubled Nigeria,

A simple troubadour with poems to share,

And a hopeful world citizen

With a precious dream, beyond compare,

Alive in Auden's luminous line:

"We must love one another or die."[2.]

NOTE 1.) sine qua non[1.] – indispensable.

2.) Auden's luminous line – SEE - September 1, 1939. W. H. Auden. <u>Another Time</u>. London: Faber and Faber, 2007. Part One. People and Places (first published, 1940) pp.103-106.

3.) Taking a break from the interminable wrestle with words, I made myself a cup of coffee and switched on the radio, after reworking the concluding lines of my poem. I found myself listening, in wonder, to the tail-end of an interview with Shirley Williams, daughter of Vera Brittain, whose First World War memoir was one of my mother's most treasured books. In 2014, a BBC and BFI film based on "Testament of Youth", was making impact, focusing attention on the meanings and legacy of that catastrophic conflict. Shirley Williams' interview ended with her quoting Auden's immortal line, the very line I had written down several minutes earlier. Later, I revised and reworked my poem, trying to make sense of what was at stake, concerning the Scottish Referendum on Independence and the Referendum on Britain's membership of the European Union. Auden's luminous line seemed never more apposite!

INTEGRITY

5th February 2015

for Andrey Kurkov, ethnic Russian and Ukrainian patriot,
not either or, mais tous les deux.

His mother-tongue, Russian,

Rich and nourishing,

His sense of nation

A Ukraine, independent,

And for his refusal, categorical,

To excise one of these twin allegiances,

Deny his right to loyalties integral,

Came words, incendiary, fired in his direction

From forces, locked in futile contention,

Demanding he submit his creative spirit,

Compliant to one reductive agenda.

His response, expressed in public and private,

Followed a path, consistent and defiant,

To be BOTH Ukrainian and Russian,

A complex, authentic identity

No crass combatants will ever take from him.

DRESDEN, FEBRUARY 1945 AND 2015, DEBALTSEVA, FEBRUARY 2015

14th February 2015

In Dresden, piety was on solemn show
To remind us what the flames of war can do,
While in cities and towns of Eastern Ukraine,
Children's lives are being blighted, beyond repair,
By weapons of war, discharging sorrow and pain
Into shattered homes, engulfed in flame,
On the orders of men, immune to shame,
Imprisoned within an imperial theme,
The curse of rivals, East and West,
Locked in their deadly game of chess.

REMEMBRANCE

17th February 2015

The Old Veteran took to the airways,
In the fading light of his closing years,
To explain why he would never march,
Uniformed and bemedalled, along streets
That would only unleash his bitter tears,
For my remembrance, he explained,
Is every day of every living year,
As I recollect and see and hear
Men, dispatched with insolent contempt
Into the abyss of meaningless death,
Belatedly labelled, glorious and blest,
To suit the army, politicians and monarchy
Betraying my brothers' untold stories,
Buried in official pomp and circumstance;
And when I speak to the young, sitting
Alert and inquisitive in their classrooms,
My voice disinters some essential truths
To protect them, from the invasive coercion
That led to the graves of my lost generation;
And should a lively listener pointedly ask:
How can we make sense of our troubled past,
When we were taught, our officer-top-brass

Were undisputed masters of the universe;
And were the Kaiser's compliant footsoldiers
Barbarian brutes, or puppet-men
Tricked and coerced into futile war games,
Disposable pawns, deployed just like us?,
I hear ghost-voices whisper in my ear,
Now don't let us down, for our sakes and theirs.
So remembrance, for me, takes the form
Of acknowledging, both what I am
And what I once unforgettably was,
My feeble failures, transforming joys
And the deep, embedded memories
Of ice-cold trenches, in desecrated earth;
But above all else, I must use
My sunset days to craft my words
And warn against the horrors of wars
Packaged in false-patriotic salestalk,
A fate I have lived, now live to expose.

WHEN WILL WE EVER LEARN?

26th February 2015

Thoughts on a tangled web of relations between Ukraine,
Russia, the U.S.A., Germany, France and Britain
AND
Memories of singing Pete Seeger's "Where Have All The
Flowers Gone", during the Vietnam War catastrophe.

The truce has been breached

As we knew it would,

Words too formal-weak

To effect change for the good;

But we're hardly surprised,

Since we've been here before

And truces, too often, fail to flower.

The truce has been breached,

The temperature rises,

The silhouettes of soldiers

Disturb the horizon.

It takes only a few generals and leaders,

Mirror image rivals, in distant locations,

To send families, scurrying numb with terror,

Into the depths of comfortless cellars,

And on the frozen faces of little children

The unspoken, angry, hopeless questions,

What did we do to deserve this horror
And why can our parents no longer protect us?
But in presidential offices and palaces
The talk is of national pride and honour,
And how to outwit and outmanoeuvre
An insatiable enemy, hungry for power.

The truce has been breached,
Still-born from the start,
War so easy to initiate,
When minds are assaulted and inflamed,
Fear-injected, passive-manipulated,
Propaganda-primed into acceptance
Of what should never have been contemplated;
And how hard are the means to bring war to an end,
When children die and parents outraged,
Turn, in despair, to acts of revenge,
Yet, each time wars of relentless attrition
Wreak devastation across generations,
Weary survivors shake solemn heads
And sagely chorus the familiar refrain,
This time, we must surely learn,
Never, never, never again,
For this is the debt the living owe,
To the blighted lives and victims of war.
And surely, as arsenals of W.M.D.[1]

Proliferate in stealth, out of control,
Our Times demand we answer the question:
Is there a future for humanunkind;
And why have we not interred
The old imperial paradigm,
Blindly followed down
Millennia of pain,
Punctuated by treacherous ceasefires
That disappear in smoke and flame?

The truce has been breached
As we knew it would,
Words too formal-weak
To effect change for the good;
But we're hardly surprised,
Since we've been here before
And truces too often fail to flower,
When, like stubborn infants, we refuse to learn
The quintessential lesson from the past
That the legacy of war
Breeds harvests of distress,
Passed from one generation to the next.

And if the only beneficiaries of war
Are the arms dealers and manufacturers,
What kind of wealth is worth possessing,

Hidden from sight in secret tax havens,

While millionaire, billionaire

Vulture, vampire expropriators

Live in walled mansions and palaces,

Security-segregated,

Luxury-incarcerated

In social apartheid,

In crazed isolation

From despoiled humanity?

NOTE – W.M.D.[1]- Weapons of Mass Destruction.

R. H. Tawney's definition of capitalism, its contradictions and dangers, informs what I have tried to articulate in this poem.

"It is that whole system of appetites and values, with its deification of the life of snatching to hoard, and hoarding to snatch, which now, in the hour of its triumph, while the plaudits of the crowd still ring in the ears of the gladiators and the laurels are still unfaded on their brows, seems sometimes to leave a taste as of ashes on the lips of a civilization which has brought to the conquest of its material environment resources unknown in earlier ages, but which has not yet learnt to master itself."

SEE - R. H. Tawney. Religion And The Rise of Capitalism. A Historical Study. London: John Murray, 1929 (1st edition, 1926), pp.286-7.

BOY SOLDIERS IN CYBERSPACE

22nd February 2015

When my friend found her Chinese guests
Playing their computer games with intense
Excitement they could barely contain,
Curious, she asked the boys to explain;
And swift as a fighter plane came the reply:
Ah, we've just completed the extermination
Of our inferior enemy, the U.S. of A.,
For China is sure to rule the world one day,
Our revenge for the humiliations
Making us look small and weak
In the black hole of our nineteenth century,
And into the twentieth, competing
Empires contending to control our destiny,
Defeats our teachers and history books
Have etched, with pain, on our nation's memory,
Reminding us to serve and protect
China's honour and sovereign territory;
But, soon, we shall be at the centre again,
Powerful and respected, where we should be.
Well, boys will be boys, came my friend's cosy cliché,
While my silent response was not laughter but fear.

When my friend found her summer vacation
Self-confident students from the U.S.A.
Playing THEIR computer games with the same
Manic supercharged energy and flair,
Naturally, she asked them to explain:
Gee, Mam, we've just deployed the latest killer U.A.V.s[1.]
To wipe our Russian rivals off the screen,
And next in line for a dose of the same,
Those upstart Chinese with their mean, sneaky tricks,
For no nation on earth should ever be seen
To outsmart Uncle Sam and the Land of the Free.
Well boys will be boys, came her cheerful reply,
As I shook my head and heaved a long sigh.

The following summer, when she hosted guests
And taught her usual English language course
To the sons of Russian plutocrats,
She anticipated their explanation
In response to her customary question,
Concerning THEIR enthusiastic addiction:
We've hacked into the Pentagon,
After lunch we'll move up to the next level
And teach those Yanks some respect for our nation,
That is, if any are left, after we've dealt with them.
We guarantee to finish the game, before
You call us for tea, because we love speed,

Just like our action-strongman, maestro-mentor,
The Great Leader of rejuvenated Mother Russia.
Well boys will be boys, the whole world over,
Came my friend's false-optimistic rejoinder.

But this time, enough was too much, so I warned her:
A war game is more than a profit spinner,
A war game is a clever, cunning device
To infiltrate, trap and manipulate
Malleable, mischievous male adolescents
Into reductive, imperial mindsets,
For the rest of their unenlightened lives.

So what would you have me do, she demanded,
Confiscate their games, have their parents complain,
Even risk my precious livelihood
By sticking my neck out and looking absurd?

Perhaps, I suggested, your lessons might include
Immersion in Ludwig's great choral symphony,
Context explained, with additional clear
Engaging historical information,
For that universal, fabulous great,
Inspired by the theme of brotherly love,
Can offer a different view of humanity;
And don't forget, on one impassioned occasion,
Beethoven tore into shreds his dedication

To a man of the people, turned traitor,
Intoxicated with the lure of exciting,
Catastrophic, imperial misadventure.
So couldn't such teaching open minds
To new perspectives and sunnier skies,
Worth a try don't you think, my friend?

I'll consider the matter; but, in any event,
You would have to come and help out, she quipped;
Thus, in the end, we reached the conclusion
Education Beyond Borders could offer
A solution with healing alternatives,
For things, we agreed, can't go on like this,
With the established world disorder
Inflicting its curse, uninvited, on all of us!
So away with divisive ideologies
Building new Berlin Walls and hostilities,
For surely, if we put our minds to it
We can do so much better than this?

CODA: Two sides of the same filthy coin
And as for the Lost Boys in cyberspace,
Let them engage with the ruptured reality
Of children their age, brutalised by war,
Dragged into horror, with nowhere to run.
Let them examine and see for themselves,

Both sides of the same filthy coin,

Rich boys and poor, robbed of their humanity,

Two sets of extremes, cursed by contrasting,

Interconnected, avoidable tragedies.

NOTE – U.A.V.s[1] – unmanned aerial vehicles

2.) Ludwig van Beethoven (1770-1827) had planned to dedicate his Third Symphony "The Eroica" (1804) to Napoléon. Disgusted and incensed by Napoléon's imperial hubris, he tore up the dedication. His Ninth Symphony, "The Choral" (1824) includes the passage from Schiller's "Ode To Joy", which became the anthem of the European Union. In December 1989, to celebrate the fall of the Berlin Wall, Leonard Bernstein was invited to conduct the Bavarian Radio Symphony Orchestra, Ludwig's Ninth to be performed on both sides of that infamous divide. For this special occasion, musicians from the U.S.S.R., U.S.A., Britain and France performed with colleagues from Berlin, Dresden and Munich. Leonard Bernstein was determined that these two concerts would celebrate both "human freedom" and "joy". He felt this was "a heaven-sent moment to sing 'Freiheit' (freedom) wherever the score indicates the word 'Freude' (joy)."

3.) Victor-Marie Hugo (1802-1885). See his poetic indictment of Napoléon's hubris, leading into the Retreat from Moscow and Battle of Waterloo. In "L'Expiation," his focus is on the tragic loss of ordinary lives, as well as the folly of imperial hubris.

"Hier la grande armée, et maintenant troupeau."

(Yesterday the Army Invincible, today a mere flock.)

THE SNOWDROPS IN THE DANE JOHN GARDENS or PITY THE CHILDREN of Syria, South Sudan, Somalia, Palestine, Nigeria, Iraq, Ukraine, Yemen, Libya...

18th February 2015

lines written after a walk through a Canterbury park.

As politicians and world leaders
Turn their minds to the business of war,
Little children cower in terror,
Misery exploding into their homes,
While the snowdrops in the Dane John Gardens
Intimations, that, slowly, spring is on its way
Fail to warm my troubled heart,
Chilled, cheerless, by the nightmare thought
Of young lives ruined, shattered and lost,
No spring will welcome or touch.
But the men, deep in consultation
With their expert military advisers,
Pour over tactics and manoeuvres,
Too preoccupied to consider
The crimes they, indirectly authorize.
So whether Russian, Ukrainian,
Western or Eastern European,
Chinese, African, Antipodean,

A U.S. or Middle Eastern citizen,
A child of strife-torn Pakistan or India,
The question that confronts each one of us
Demands an urgent, thoughtful answer:
To what kind of dangerous misleaders
Do we blindly cede such lethal powers;
And why do we cling to myths, ancient and modern,
Rooted in political disfunction,
That render impossible a better tomorrow?
So while the snowdrops in the Dane John Gardens
Offer glimpses of light in a gloomy dark,
As long as children are tossed into oblivion,
So long will spring remind me of saplings
Axed and felled, never to feel the warmth
Of sun-kissed buds, bursting into flower;
And, surely, careless leaders, promoting war
Should be the first, to taste its fury and horror,
Instead of visiting random outrage
On the voiceless, vulnerable-dispossessed,
Their lives, extinguished in instants, casual-explosive,
Some corpses, with brave defiance, retrieved in haste,
Interred in perfunctory, makeshift graves,
Other victims, rubble-buried, fractured, dying,
Amid bodies left to rot, exposed, abandoned
By grief-stricken families, their homes razed

Haphazard into jagged fragments,
Innocents, fleeing zealots on streets anarchic,
And from merciless skies, punitive bombardments
No cocooned, public-relations-camouflaged,
Metropolitan politician, general
Or highly paid expert adviser
Would take the time or trouble to grieve over,
For high-tech war has its own momentum,
With scant concern for civilian victims.
In Canterbury, the supermarkets
Will soon display, rows of chocolate eggs
For parents to hide in suburban gardens,
While in Syria, bombs in assorted sizes
That rain down, ruthless, from threatening skies,
Shower horror and hurt on children's lives.
Why are some children, carefully
Protected, petted and pampered,
While others, deemed unfortunate,
Expendable commodities
Or disregarded, uncounted casualties?
As long as children are tossed,
Contemptuous into oblivion,
So long will Spring's longed-for arrival
Breed demands insistent, for change essential.
The snowdrops in the Dane John Gardens,

Points of light in a gloomy dark,
Remind us of nature's prodigious beauty,
Remind us, we have made ourselves
Prisoners of insatiable greed,
Delusional obsessions, fickle fantasies
That scar the earth, our home,
Leaving us myopic losers,
Lost in time, divided, alone.

FROM THE MOUTHS OF BABES

May 2016

for Barbara, Helen and Guillaume.
North Carolina 1998, Paris 2015, Canterbury 2016.

PART I

North Carolina 1998.

It must have been the reference to god
Which stuck stubborn, in that six-year-old throat,
Causing the teacher in charge of her class
To stare astonished, dumbfounded, nonplussed,
For it was to her, beyond credulity
That any elementary pupil
Would refuse to place hand on heart
And salute the greatest nation on earth,
By pledging allegiance to the flag,
Every morning, before classes began;
But there she stood, head down, non-compliant,
No pledge emanating from her tight-lipped mouth,
A mystery to be penetrated,
Investigated, eliminated,
Like a virulent weed, rooted out,
Lest contagion breed unpatriotic thoughts
And Mrs Carey blamed for harbouring

Subversive sedition among her charges,
Landing her in a witch-hunt of gross suspicions,
Led by her zealous pastor and head teacher.
Digging and delving with utmost discretion,
Mrs C. assumed the rôle of detective,
Starting from the scandalous rumour
That Helen and the rest of her family
Abstained form church, on a permanent basis.
Careful questioning proved, beyond doubt,
That Caroline Carey was on the right path,
For pastor, priest, vicar, minister,
Each in turn, confirmed the family's
Polite indifference to the local
All-pervasive Christian ethos,
While the parents' concerns over climate
Change, growing inequality,
Environmental degradation
Smacked of suspect socialist intentions.
Well, after all, they're Brits, capable
Of underhand tricks with allies and friends,
Yet, when in a fix, to us, they come begging,
Calling on American Exceptionalism,
Mused an increasingly angry Caroline.
Asked to conform to her teacher's demand,
Helen, polite-persistent, shook her head.

I can't promise what I don't understand;
And anyway, at home, we don't believe in god;
And Mummy and Daddy have told me
Not to tell lies, or make promises
I know are empty and will never keep anyway.

Mrs Carey paused in stunned, reluctant
Admiration, for Helen's courage
Touched her heart, as the child stood waiting,
Averting her eyes, pride concealing tears
Deep inside, a little girl, taunted and teased,
Questioned by classmates, jeering, unkind,
Shouting in her face, she was the devil's child.
A summit was convened, with Helen,
Her parents, Mrs Carey and the Head.
After a voicing of views in collision,
A compromise concluded the meeting.
Helen was allowed to stand in silence
During the prescribed, daily recitation;
But for her part, she accepted to place
Her small right hand on her beating heart,
Signalling her membership of the class
To which, for a while, she continued to belong.

Later, her mother confided to a friend,
Well you see, we come from Yorkshire,

Where folk don't like to be pushed around,
So I'm not surprised our Helen defended
Her dignity and pride, under attack
From a string of nasty, cutting remarks
Kept for some time, buried deep inside,
A little girl encouraged at home, to think
For herself and balance natural wonder
With probing questions and rational thought;
And as for the position she took,
In that conformist North Carolina school,
It seems to me that, in essence, it was
A testimony to the family she loves,
An insistence on honest loyalty,
And a polite refusal to succumb
To regulations that stuck in her throat.

NOTE – Herewith the lines that stuck in a certain six-year-old throat:

The Pledge Of Allegiance

"I pledge allegiance to the Flag of the United States of America and to the Republic for which it stands; One Nation under God indivisible, with Liberty and Justice for all."

14th June, 1954.

PART II

At first, Guillaume fell under the spell
Of Delphine Delcourt's sophistication,
Her witty tales of peregrinations
Across the United States of America,
During her year of total immersion
In Ivy League élite presumption,
Filling her with boundless enthusiasm
For the chic-stupendous optimism
Of young entrepreneurs, pursuing dreams
At high-tech speed, ready to innovate,
Honed to compete, hungry-determined to succeed;
And this unfettered admiration
Rippled electric throughout the classroom,
A Hollywood-magic infatuation,
Transmitted from teacher to bedazzled pupils,
While under Delphine's carefully acquired
Bostonian accent, lurked dismissive
Irritation with Madame Dupont's
Ancien Régime teaching methods,
Insisting her pupils learn to speak
English with Received Pronunciation,
Oxford and Cambridge, her reference points,

For the school children in her charge, belonged
To distinguished Parisien social circles.
Delphine's earnest eradication
Of her predecessor's outmoded,
Exasperating indoctrination,
Provided wholesale initiation
Into the breezy, can-do informality
Accompanying the ideology
Of success and power across the Atlantic;
And so, she asked Guillaume's class
To learn the Pledge of Allegiance by heart,
A sure way to promote and enhance
Liaisons amicales, between the U.S, and France.
Guillaume asked why the English, Madame Dupont
Had taught, was in disgrace, out of favour
And why they were now expected to change
From British to U.S. accents and spelling,
Because came Delphine's quick-fire response
The U.S.A. is a republic, like ours,
Founded on the purest principles of
Liberty, Unity and Justice for all.
Now Guillaume, a lad fourteen-years-old,
Was endowed with an irrepressible,
Alert, inquisitive yearning for truth.
Something, he thought, is not quite right,

Britain can't be so démodé and bad,
Nor the U.S.A. quite so golden-shiny-bright;
But like a good pupil, he did his homework,
And learned those patriotic lines by heart,
Though something still seemed to stick in his throat.
Surfing the Net before going to bed,
Guillaume explored two words, mixed up in his head:
Guantánamera and Guantánamo.
The first, belonged to a song, his Spanish
Teacher had recently played and sung;
Ah, how he wanted to hear those words again,
Words to savour, explore and retain.
But what of the second, where did it come from,
And how had it lodged in his teeming brain?
Did that word, less musical, somehow sharper
Come from something his father had said,
Something half-heard, then quickly forgotten?
The first, an anthem of celebration,
Dedicated to struggling humanity,
The second, a byword for injustice,
Torture, never-ending incarceration,
Two worlds, connected and disconnected,
Two words, two concepts at loggerheads.
Guillaume shut down his computer, tearful,
Distressed, angry at the very existence

Of searchlit cells and the Black-Hole-Horror
Of Justice assaulted, raped, dishonoured.
So how to recite that Pledge with the others
Tomorrow, in school, before Delphine Delcourt?
The lady arrived with a U.S. flag,
Because, she chuckled, let's do it authentic;
I'll stand at the front, with the Stars and Stripes,
Right hand on heart, just follow my lead,
As I hear you recite those powerful lines.
Now imagine you're in junior high,
Starting the school-day, like regular guys.
Guillaume's hands hung stiff on each side,
His mouth clamped shut, anger in his eyes.
Well, thought Delphine, there's always
One who won't comply
And turning to the culprit,
demanded to know why...

Last night, I discovered a horrible truth,
So I can't say that Pledge, though I learnt it by heart,
Until Black-Hole-Guantánamo is closed down
And the prisoners freed from Camp X-ray,
Where Justice is daily mocked and outlawed.
Today, in that terrible cruel place,
The Stars and Stripes flutter in the breeze,
So I choose silence, out of respect

For men treated like slaves and left to rot.
This is my pledge to teacher and class,
These are the lines I offer you all,
Though they may be hard to listen to.

Guillaume stood in silence, his heart was pounding,
Then a few of his classmates started clapping.
Well I never, exclaimed Mademoiselle Delcourt
You've made your point and there's much to discuss,
Now open your books, so class can commence.
Non, mes amis, she held up her hand,
Discussion is postponed for a later date,
So please settle down, we need to get on.

Guillaume was nothing, if not persistent;
He discussed the matter with his Dad that evening;
And Dad suggested his son download
A copy of William Blake's "Jerusalem."
Just in case Mlle Delcourt has a lapse of memory,
Guillaume Blake's poem might come in handy
For lively discussion and comparison.
By the way, in what you said, at school today,
I hear the echo of "Guantánamera,"
The clear voice of "un hombre sincero,"
Feeling, thinking at one with "el pueblo";
And though your teacher is annoyed, perturbed,

Your Father is proud of the courage you showed

And the careful courtesy that clothed your words.

Never forget, his Dad concluded,

There's good and bad in every nation;

And our belovèd France is no exception.

What the world needs now are global citizens,

Another idea to present to your teacher;

But choose your timing, proceed with discretion;

And first, prepare what you want to say in English;

And I wouldn't spend too much time, worrying

About choice of accent and pronunciation,

Concentrate first on vocabulary and grammar!

Guillaume laughed and wondered how many friends

Had dads as charming-provocative as his!

NOTE – In these poems I have combined British and U.S. English with occasional words and phrases from French and Spanish, because so many words contain a specific cultural significance, a rich unique resonance that defies translation. It is a good thing to learn several languages, because this allows us to visit other cultures; and all cultures, all languages, belong within the human family.

Below his English translation of Pablo Neruda's magnificent poem "El Pueblo," Alastair Reid comments:

"The word 'pueblo' invokes in Spanish much more than either a place or the people who inhabit it: It humanizes a place as a state of being, as a set of values and allegiances. English has nothing quite as embracing."

SEE – The Essential Neruda. Selected Poems, edited by Mark Eisner. Hexham: Bloodaxe Books Ltd. 2010, p.165.

FATHER, SON AND THE SPIRIT OF DANCE

25th December 2015

for Carlos and Pedro Acosta.

Disciplined explosion of limbs in motion,
Commanding attention, dancing for a nation,
The spirit of Cuba fiery and bold,
Alive on a London stage, for the whole world.
How far he had come from football obsession
And nascent, confused gangster inclinations.
At the start of his odyssey, a young boy
Of the barrios, rebellious and wild,
With a father, stern-strong at his side,
Setting his son on a radical course
A boarding ballet school, no ifs or buts,
Where the lad could flourish in more fertile soil
Than the survival-struggle at home would allow.
Later, the father commanded his son,
When you realise your dream in London town,
Though sometimes your spirit droops in homesick gloom,
Remember, the strength-and-beauty you express
Is not for you alone, but for all of us:
Family, friends and the land of your birth.

Seventeen years later, the time had come
To honour his father's formidable love
And bring back to Cuba all he had learned,
For a new dream had taken root in his soul,
To create with his brothers and sisters
A company, innovative, eclectic,
In a sunny Caribbean setting,
Inviting, mesmerizing, retaining
World audiences' joyful attention;
And this, perhaps his greatest dream,
Emanated from the man who taught him,
Art belongs to all of us, its seeds
Lie dormant in every living soul;
But for those seeds to flourish and grow,
There must be fertile, nourishing soil
And, at times, to bring great dreams to fruition
You must venture afar and brave storm after storm.

AND STILL HE SINGS

11th September 2013

for Joan Jara, Manuela and Amanda.

He sang for social justice
And his songs spoke to the people's needs;
He performed in the favelas,
Knowing that for so many
Grand concert halls were out of reach;
On the airwaves, his words carried
A vision, radical and brave,
A transfer of wealth and power
Through peaceful, democratic means;
And for this, his hands were smashed,
His voice outlawed and silenced
On the orders of state terrorists,
Busy torturing dreams, destroying lives,
Egged on from complicit sidelines
By their Stateside-compañeros-in-crime.

Today, forty years after tyranny's
Triumph, the memories are strong;
The reckoning, essential, still goes on,
While the music of Victor Jara
Is celebrated and sung,

Restored to the People

Where it rightfully belongs,

For you[1] cannot chain melodies

That carry Freedom's Song;

And though you murdered with impunity,

He will live in his music

Long after you have gone,

A dirty footnote in history

To remind Chile's children

Of lessons that must be learned.

NOTE – You[1]: the reference is to the plural form of the pronoun, i.e. all those who participated in and prolonged the terror unleashed by Augusto Pinochet and the Chicago Boys, those who teach and propagate the ideological orthodoxies of the Chicago School of Economics, whose principle founder "Milton Friedman, grand guru of the movement for unfettered capitalism," also referred to as "radical free-market economics," argued that "governments must remove all rules and regulations standing in the way of the accumulation of profits… sell off any assets… that corporations could be running at a profit" and "dramatically cut back the funding of social programmes." Naomi Klein has demonstrated the global reach of Friedman's antidemocratic fundamentalism and the savage effects of "disaster capitalism," wedded to the theory and practice of unregulated and deregulated commerce.

SEE – The Shock Doctrine. Naomi Klein. London: Penguin Books, 2007, p.4, p.51, pp.56-57 and pp.441-442.

Victor Jara was an early casualty of the 1973 coup d'état against the democratically-elected, socialist Government of Chile's Salvador Allende, smashing his hands, an act of unspeakable, choreographed violence against a much-loved guitarist, composer, singer-songwriter and supporter of Allende's socialist initiatives. Victor's murder was clearly designed to send a message to the public, instilling fear and imposing silence, since his music was loved and appreciated by the general public. The crimes committed against Victor Jara epitomize the most extreme forms of censorship and violation imaginable. Countless victims endured comparable fates. After the end of Pinochet's reign of terror, Victor's music and legacy were resurrected, reinstated as national treasures and a foundation was established in his name.

For many world citizens there are two infamous nine elevens: that of 1973 and the attack on the World Trade Centre in New York, some twenty eight years later. On the 11th September, 2013, I had been thinking of both atrocities and their consequences. Tuning in to the B.B.C. World Service, serendipity brought me half of an interview with Victor's widow, Joan. Up to this point, I had wrongly assumed she was either North or South American, but discovered her nationality to be British. At the end of the interview, I sat down and wrote this poem for Victor, his widow and two daughters. I would have liked a certain Lady Thatcher to have listened to that interview and reflected on its moving dignity and significance.

I also remember that shortly after the World Trade Centre attack, on the side of our former post office in Canterbury City centre (now a fast food restaurant), someone had graffitied in capital letters "REMEMBER THE OTHER 9/11."

ALIENATION

20th February 2017

While the world's Superpowers, in haste, turn
Their backs on those, conveniently relabelled,
Downgraded and objectified,
As inconsequential "collateral damage,"
On the Dark-Net, Daesh advances with speed,
Cruelty and terror, recolonizing
Outraged hearts, from computer screens
In homes and bedrooms, across the World,
Images, grotesque-ripe, for transformation
Into asymmetric, murderous deeds,
Invading young minds, angry, frustrated,
Questioning their sense of alienation,
In countries, where they remain rejected,
Though by birthright, classified native.
In homes and bedrooms across the World,
The Young see civilizations ripped apart,
Ancient cultures, torn asunder,
By forces global, regional, local,
As conflicts spiral out of control.
In such conditions, contradictions,
How can our Children blossom and bloom,
When their sense of belonging is stolen, broken

By Lords of Misrule, addicted to power,
Looting the planet, sanity abandoned,
In corrupting, compulsive, explosive
Death-dealing games of divide-to-rule?
I recognize, as my sister, my brother,
All who dare to live lives of principled
Opposition to such a dehumanizing,
Hate-inculcating system;
They will be my compañeros siempre,
Regardless of skin colour,
Cultural variation,
Skills and occupation
And certified country of origin.
The root is one; au fond mes amis,
We belong to the same human family.
Let prejudice be dismantled,
Interred in the rubble
Of demolished border walls;
Let the hands of friendship
Defeat the bloody arms of war,
For now the dangers are too great to ignore,
At risk our very survival, uncertain,
Hanging, precarious, in the balance,
Time and the planet losing patience
With our wilful refusal to emerge

From primitive-crude[1] mental conditioning,

Thinking ourselves sophisticated-clever,

With enough W.M.D.[2] to destroy

Not just one, but multiple worlds;

And if foreign visitors from different galaxies,

Have ventured, in secret, to our shores

And continents, I would hazard a guess

Their response, unequivocal, would have been

To head home with accelerating velocity,

Having glimpsed the mess we insist on making.

Though inventors, too often

We kill creativity,

Ignoring the fact, we are but one

Link, in the great, evolving,

Magnificent chain of being.

I recognize, as my sister, my brother,

All who dare to live lives of principled

Opposition to such a dehumanizing system;

They will be my compañeros siempre,

Their determination, unshakeable,

Bringing light into dark places,

Across continents and generations.

NOTE – primitive-crude[1] -here the idea of primitive is associated with the acquisitive-destructive mentality of high-tech, predatory capitalist societies. More than 170 years ago, Chief Seattle, leader of one of the Northwest Native American Nations, foresaw the dangers of social fragmentation and environmental devastation, when he spoke warning words of ignored wisdom to the expansionist Government in Washington, D.C., determined to buy his People's land, the very concept of buying and selling land, both blasphemous and alien to his People:

"...My ancestors said to me, This we know:
The earth does not belong to us. We belong to the earth.
The voice of my grandmother said to me,
Teach your children what you have been taught.
The earth is our mother.
What befalls the earth befalls all the sons and
Daughters of the earth..."
"...This we know: All things are connected
Like the blood that unites us.
We did not weave the web of life,
We are merely a strand in it.
Whatever we do to the web, we do to ourselves."

Now in 2017, one hundred and seventy five years later, we hear and see the Sioux People struggling to protect their land, habitat and water, against threats from an aggressive U.S. Oil Industry, exercising direct influence on the new Federal Government. President Trump has lost no time in rescinding his predecessor's Executive Order, protecting the historical rights of the Sioux in the state of North Dakota, from the potentially catastrophic depredations of sophisticated, high-tech, corporate capitalism. Chief Seattle's speech never more relevant, should be mandatory reading for all concerned.

SEE – Brother Eagle, Sister Sky. A message from Chief Seattle. Paintings by Susan Jeffers. London: Picture Puffins, 1993, passim.

W.M.D.[2]- Weapons of Mass Destruction.

THREE POEMS FOR THE CHILDREN OF WAR-TORN SYRIA

25th June 2014

AN IMAGE INSISTS

A boy of twelve moves slow-fast-deliberate,
A bouquet of factory-farmed roses
Resting, dried-blood red, in his patient arms,
While cars, guilty-indifferent, speed past,
Quick to avoid acquaintance with his loss
And touch the cruelty of those captive roses,
Wilting weary under unkind sun,
He must, smiling, salestalk singly, one-by-one
Into food-money for his family
Waiting, refugee-forlorn in their rented room,
A child, missile-flung into a father's rôle,
His eyes, brown-velvet pools of infinite sorrow,
Stare stoïcal-numb before the eight hours
Or ten of walking-hawking sterile blooms,
So that his family will not sleep, yet again,
On empty-growling stomachs and gnawing distress,
While cushioned opulent, on the proceeds
From political thuggery and arms deals,
Tyrants and warmongers disdain to consider

The random horror hurtling, exploding,

Missile-monstrous on the lives of children,

Limbs, homes, families, dreams broken,

Their present destroyed, their future stolen,

So the most beautiful rose, bought and sold

In the money markets of the world

Is not the hothouse flower of insolent power,

But the rose offered by a young son

To help feed his family and father;

And in these lines, his story rises

Because an image of beauty, pain and wonder

Insisted, persisted, would not be ignored

Until accorded the recognition

Its simple honour surely deserves.

NOTE – I would like to acknowledge the influence of Christopher Okigbo's poem, "Siren Limits IV," especially, the first verse:

> An image insists
> From flagpole of the heart;
> Her image distracts
> With the cruelty of the rose...

Change "her" to "his" in the third line and this verse evokes the enduring impact on me, of a brief interview on British television with a Syrian boy of twelve, selling roses on the busy streets near his temporary Lebanese refugee home, because his unemployed father could not find work and, in desperation, had turned for help and support to his young son, in whose utterances not one word of complaint to the journalist and in whose beautiful eyes, I saw a mixture of infinite sorrow and tender love; and so, for the best part of two months this image persisted; and only when I resumed "the interminable wrestle with words" (T. S. Eliot's succinct definition of the poet's vocation), did I find a small measure of temporary relief.

I wish Messrs Putin, Assad, Rouhani, Obama, Hollande, Cameron and other world and regional leaders from Saudi Arabia, Iraq, the U.A.E., Qatar, Kuwait, Jordan, Turkey, Greece and Lebanon… could be made to watch and respond to that interview with hearts and minds, for the meaning therein is timeless and universal. In this instance, the child is, indeed, father to the man.

At present, there are estimated to be one million Syrian children who have been made refugees on account of the civil war blighting their native land; and the U.N.H.C.R. has less than one third of the funding required to provide the barest essentials to displaced Syrian refugees.

SEE – <u>Labyrinths</u>. Christopher Okigbo. London: Heinemann African Writers Series, 1971, p.27.

SMALL BOY WITH HUGE HEART

21st September 2015

for the children of Syria, the hospitable citizens of
München and Channel 4 reporter, Matt Frei.

Such a small boy, weaving determined
His perilous path, through a multitude
Of noise-in-motion, a tidal surge
Of straining limbs, outstretched hands
Reaching for the food München[1] Volunteers,
Warm of heart, had hastened to provide.

Such a small boy, seeming alone,
In such a throng of desperate souls,
Frail-strong, intent on sustaining his own
Momentum steady, as he weaved
His way hazardous to reach his goal,
A minnow in a shark-infested world.

The foreign correspondent's camera
Tracked, intermittent, sporadic sightings
Of this diminutive dodger, diving
Through the crush of towering throngs,
For no hand, elbow, foot or vicious boot
Would distract this Kindlein[2] from what he had to do.

At last, the journalist, happy, exclaimed:
Success has crowned his effort in the end.
See those tiny hands clutch that bowl of food,
More precious to him than diamonds or gold;
Now, surely, he must seek a quieter space
To savour his moment of triumph
Amid cruel, commonplace distress.

But soon the reporter's words faltered,
Trickling slow, like astonished tears,
When he saw the child approach a figure
Huddled in black, sitting by the roadside,
Then kneel to offer her that precious food.
She must, she has to be his mother:
This, surely, the simple explanation
For this unexpected situation.

Then the reporter's voice fell silent,
For what words could carry and convey
The measure of this little boy's love
For his mother, careworn beyond despair.
A little child, not more than six years old,
Has wordless, challenged the cruelty
Of depraved men with hearts of stone,
Reminding us, once more, of the pressing need
To relearn the most important lesson of all.

<u>NOTE</u> – München[1] - Munich

Kindlein[2] - the diminutive form of the German word das Kind, meaning small child.

THE ABANDONED

10th February 2016

A refugee boy in Lebanon
Twelve years old, lonely-forlorn,
Toils in a brick factory,
Should be at school,
His education stolen,
Wonders, in vain, why barrel bombs
And over-zealous Russian planes
Roared with apocalyptic fire and brimstone
To destroy his life and demolish his home;
Asks himself if presidents, pilots, generals,
Members of that other drone-active
Murky-mysterious coalition,
And those wild warrior-men with murderous eyes
Have any notion of just what they are doing.
He wonders if his hard-won-puny contribution
Will help fund treatment for his baby brother's
Fast deteriorating cancer condition,
Though he keeps his counsel to himself,
Avoiding the pain in his father's eyes,
Since the day he saw that father cry
Tears of shame and humiliation,
Grieving, helpless, for his family and nation.

Limbs aching, heart frozen, mind numb,

The boy imagines the life chances, burnished bright,

The sons of armchair-warrior presidents

Take for granted and claim as their birthright,

As he asks in silence, what have I done

To be sentenced to hell, excluded from their club?

If I survive, should I not heed the call

To arm myself and take revenge on them all?

But that is a recipe, he already knows

Will only serve to perpetuate

The hell he is living, hates and deplores,

A fate he would not inflict on any living soul.

Still, he wishes he could be afforded

The chance, to ask those demon-monster-men,

Responsible for his family's pain,

What they would do, if their sons met his fate

And why do their hearts contain so much hate?

NOTE – To date, the population of fragile Lebanon has increased by a quarter, due to the influx of desperate Syrian refugees.

Recently, a friend asked me, 'Hilary, why don't you pen more cheerful poems?' My explanation lacked the concentrated power of Russia's national poet, addressing this very issue.

For a poet
Even disaster
Is on the agenda.
Alexander Sergeyevich Pushkin (1799-1837)
In our troubled times, I would go further:

For a poet, today
Disaster must
Be part of the agenda,
The need to speak
Truth to power
Greater than ever.

THEFT, CORPORATE-STYLE

18th December 2014

The corporations, defiling our world
Extract their profits from the poorest on earth,
Pitiless in their promiscuous plunder
Of ocean, land and human endeavour,
As a bonny, brave Indonesian boy
Toils by the side of the father he loves,
Though the father would rather salvage his life
From the devastation of illegal tin mines,
Where death hurtles down from cruel landslides;
He repeats, time and time again,
I must send you to school, save you from this hell;
But the child of twelve, with insistent calm,
Refuses to leave his father's side
And labours long, relentless hours,
Washing the tin his father has mined,
His love, a quiet, constant companion
To the adult man, casually enslaved
To feed the greed of a system depraved.

THE FEAST OF FRUSTRATION

Kent, England

Supergran Barbara had had enough
Of her grandsons' shrieks and scuffles,
Their infuriating, anarchic
Food smearings and random scatterings,
Spoiling the sumptuous lunchtime feast,
She had prepared for them as a special treat.
Watching them grabbing, gobbling and gorging,
Before jumping up and down to mash their crumbs,
Into her brand-new carpet, under their feet,
Like demented puppies off the lead,
And with a stomach and head ache on the way,
She knew her response had to be quick and tough,
For mere words would fail, however sharp and rough,
So seizing, wielding her witch's magic wand
And swinging her thurible with the other hand,
She determined to transform those troublesome
Darlings, without delay, into young owlets,
Telling them it was time to fly away,
For at least a year and half a day,
And learn some decent table manners,
Before she would consider reversing her decision

And restore them, chastened, to their human condition.
"But," said the eldest, with his irrepressible grin,
As Supergran was about to exchange
The brothers' powers of shout-and-shriek
For a more subdued, owl-like, hoot-and-tweet,
"If I like flying and the freedom of the skies,
I might not want to come back, at all,
To my life full of tests and extra classes,
To prove to the world I'm as clever as Daddy is,"
And scratching his head, he concluded with glee,
"If I choose wings-and-beak over hands-and-feet,
I wouldn't need table manners to eat and drink!"
By now, enough had become too much,
And for a few brief moments, Barbara
Was pleased she had implemented her threat;
But after some time, and it didn't take long,
Supergran questioned the wisdom of what she had done,
For those rascals had turned punishment
Into unexpected freedom and fun.
"The trouble with you boys," Barbara sighed
"Is that your wits and tricks are slippery-slick."
So after some time, and it didn't take long,
Supergran questioned the wisdom of her plan;
And with another wave of her witch's wand,
The owls were turned back, into boisterous boys.

"Now clear up the mess and be quick about it,
That's why I've restored your hands, feet and legs,
For it's high time your Supergran had a rest!"

THREE POEMS FOR OUR BELEAGUERED NATIONAL HEALTH SERVICE

8th January 2011

For the late Claire Rayner, who vowed shortly before her death last year, that her spirit would return to haunt the present occupant of Number Ten, should further damage and destruction be inflicted on her beloved N.H.S.

WARNING

OR
No, you can't.
Oh yes, but we did!
So, don't undo!

Have we forgotten, so soon, so fast that

Ministers of state on our debt-ridden shores,

Schooled in the horrors of an unwanted War,

Undaunted by financial constraints,

Or murky, malevolent

Monetarist complaints,

Were once resolved, to forge a better deal

For the general welfare

Of the Common People

And our battered realm?

Without the inspirational,

Doggèd-determined Nye Bevan,
At a time of severe austerity weathering,
Would we have seen the creation
Of a sound public health system
Designed to serve ALL the citizens
Of a modestly self-confident nation,
Struggling to stitch the wounds
Of ancient, sterile class division?
Were he with us, here today,
He would thunder and roar,
"Don't let those profiteers
Sneak in through the back door
To defile, dishonour and destroy
All that we cherish, fought and Laboured for!"

PROFIT OVER PATIENTS or
PATIENTS OVER PROFIT

16th February 2011

(The choice remains OURS, though time may be
running out.) for the late Dr David Cyril Owen James, a
Welshman unstinting in his devotion and service to the
N.H.S., and a bone marrow transplant pioneer.

The queue curled serpentine around the street,

The air buzzing and humming electric,

Chatter tumbling and tripping off tongues,

Praising the change that had just begun,

Thanks to a Welsh miner's firebrand son,

With a secular mission, monumental and strong:

Free healthcare from cradle to grave for everyone,

Funded by taxation and the national purse,

A ray of sunny hope in dull, grey times

Lighting up the sky of North Kensington

And all the poor boroughs of our struggling nation.

Who would have thought we'd see the day,

When even the humblest, on the lowest wage,

Would be able to seek medical aid,

Hold his head high and be within his rights,

Without having to agonize, between

Food on the table, a blazing coal fire

To keep part of the damp-draughty house warm,

A new pair of winter boots or overdue visit
To the doctor's cough-congested waiting room?

Rumour had flown into every home
That Clem[1] and Nye[2] had even agreed
To improve the health of North Kensington
By issuing free prescriptions to everyone.
So the queues, curling noisily down the street,
Were charged with a celebratory spirit,
A festival of inspiring, smiling hope
At just what can be achieved,
With the right men and women in the lead.

Not all doctors welcomed this birth
Some scratched their heads, plotted and planned
To sabotage this visionary project
And bring it crashing, broken to the ground,
Fearing their affluent standard of living,
Professional status and social position
Would spiral down, in disastrous decline.
Dr Charles Spenser-Smith snarled through his teeth,
"These acts of vandalism, we must resist.
Why if care is not, immediately, taken
And on this, I'm sure I'm not mistaken,
Soon the charwoman, who cleans our house,
Will expect to be served by my own dear spouse!

That rabble-rouser Bevan is beyond the pale,
A dangerous socialist, better off in gaol
Than inciting the cloth-capped lower orders,
To rise above their allotted station
And challenge those born to rule over them!"

Dr Spenser-Smith felt the call to arms,
Summoned his colleagues, in haste,
To tell them in no uncertain terms,
"We must rise to the challenge
Or see our authority eroded,
Our modus vivendi threatened, destroyed;
And once we're reduced to hirelings of the state,
Do you really think the salaries paid
Will suffice to unlock and open the doors
Of the privileged clubs, where we belong,
As professional, independent Englishmen?
A little sabotage will not be out of place
To save us all, from such humiliating disgrace!"

So prescriptions of every possible description
Were written in supreme haste and derision,
From throat lozenges to laxatives,
Vapour rubs, cough mixtures, bandages,
Plasters, poultices and aspirins.
"This way," winked the doctor with a wicked grin,

"There's no escape, we're sure to win
And bring the system tumbling down,
Before it can really get off the ground!"
But a brave medical student, talking to the crowd,
Soon understood what those doctors were about;
And was equally determined it should not be allowed.
A delegation of angry patients
Decided to call on their local M.P.
And present national journalists
And local reporters, with evidence
Incontrovertible, for the whole world to see,
Exposing the tricks of saboteurs,
Intent on derailing the bold attempt
To create a fairer society for all,
A fitting, if partial, antidote
To the recent trauma and horrors of War.

Sixty three years have come and gone,
Since the battle, for the N.H.S. birth
And survival, was fiercely fought and won;
But the predators, in the shadows,
Still discharge their poisoned arrows,
Forever plotting, on the prowl, to steal
This jewel from the People's crown,
And drive decency and justice out of town.
Surely, our ancestors deserve greater respect

Than to see their efforts dealt a death-blow,

So that U.S. style private medicine

Can be invited to invade our shores,

Encouraged by the sons of Charles Spenser-Smith,

Promoting privileged access to private health care,

Profit over People, the undisclosed agenda

They seek to reinstate, at the centre, again,

While the needs of the uninsured

Are first devalued, then despised,

Rejected and ultimately ignored,

Taking us back, to where we once were, before

The years, when a Welsh miner's firebrand son

Achieved his mission, in the face of such

Maliciously orchestrated opposition.

Free health care, from cradle to grave,

For every, single living individual

Is the cornerstone of civilization,

Without which, cracks will soon appear,

Fissures in a shifting foundation,

Creating a climate of fear and regression,

What was best, once admired in our culture,

Devalued and thrown to marauding vultures.

NOTE – Clem[1]- Clement Atlee (1883-1967). As Prime Minister
in the post war (Old) Labour Government, he was responsible for

initiating the inception of the Welfare State now seriously under threat.

Nye[2]- Aneurin Bevan (1897-1960), pioneer of the National Health Service. He was opposed to increased "defence" spending at the expense of investment in the Health Service. He also fought for decent public housing and initiated a massive building programme, arguing, with his customary passionate fervour, that working class people, the backbone of the nation, deserved to live in council homes, where the rooms were of a decent size and the children had gardens to play in.

"When Britain was officially bankrupt at the end of the Second World War, the Government built its greatest public institutions, such as the National Health Service and the arts edifices of London's South Bank."

SEE - "Direct Action: There is no other way." John Pilger. New Statesman, 8th November 2010, p.21.

The fictitious anonymous medical student in my poem represents those in the medical profession, who challenged and opposed the tactics of saboteurs, represented by the fictitious Dr Charles Spenser-Smith. The over-prescription incident in North Kensington took place in 1948, following the difficult birth of the N.H.S. Similar acts of sabotage occurred throughout the nation. Nye Bevan warned that the N.H.S. would survive and thrive, as long as there were enough People ready to defend it and fight for it.

A TWO TIERED SYSTEM or
TIME IS MONEY

22nd February 2011

for Barbara.

He arrived early, fragile, nervous.
He arrived late, in bustling haste,
Making it clear, he had no time to waste,
Casting a cold, cursory glance
Over the list of pre-op patients
To be evaluated and assessed,
With his consultant's proud expertise
And swift, streamlined public service speed.

The eye surgeon signalled the procedure
Would be routine, nor last over-long,
But timely, before further damage
To his retina could possibly occur.
Unnerved by anxiety,
His listener felt so alone,
While the surgeon, quick off the mark,
Brisk and brusque, was keen to be gone,
Had no time for further questions
From this annoying, mumbling moron.
But determined, the shy, hesitant patient
Plucked up courage and pressed on,

For he needed to ascertain
That all vital information
About his connective tissue complication
Had reached the great man, and would remain
Carefully locked and stored for reference,
In his superior, brilliant, medical brain,
And the notes, computer-stored,
Essential data, at his disposal.

The surgeon paused on his way to the door,
"You should know that as an N.H.S. patient,
I have given you more than your due.
Five-to-ten minutes is the allotted time
I am duty-bound to devote to you,
After completing my pre-op assessment
And outlining what I propose to do."
He glanced at his watch, with an air distracted,
Then his fierce demeanour, seemed to soften
For an instant, as he continued:
"But should you wish to consult me some more,
My private clinic is at your disposal,
The fees I charge, moderate and reasonable,
Unlike the bloated millions, those football
Celebrities, self-regarding, demand as their due.
My secretary is available to take
Your call, so think it over, it's up to you.

Now do excuse me, I'm running late
Trying to catch up with a punishing schedule
And an excess of commitments to attend to!"

The operation was NOT a success,
In fact as the G.P. privately confessed
"The wrong procedure was applied,
The result it cannot be denied:
A botched job and a bloody mess,
Causing untold damage and deep distress.
If only the surgeon had been informed,
Why his loss of sight might not have occurred."

His widowed mother grieved and moaned,
"If I had known, if I had only been told,
I would have booked that consultation,
Even if it meant selling the pearl necklace
My husband bought for me, decades ago,
When I was still a romantic, sentimental girl
And not a frustrated mother, full of woe!"

Invocation.
I invoke the spirits of Attlee,
Bevan, Rayner and Co.
To haunt the Occupant of Number Ten,
Until he and his team do far better,
For the misguided fools who voted them in!

LOVE BEYOND BORDERS

1st September 2016

for Celia and Win.

Her hand dips into the bag on her lap,
Her flock, fluttering eager at her feet,
A congregation of courtiers,
Heads bobbing with excitement as they eat.
Who is this mysterious lady of the park,
Dispensing her bounty all the year round,
From the wheeled machine, where she sits confined,
Yet exerting her independence with pride,
A woman grounded, smiling as she feeds the birds,
Those winged wonders, born to fly, free to soar?
Come rain, come shine, autumn chill or winter gloom,
The lady proves loyal to the birds she loves.
Before she has barely entered the park,
They gather, waiting, cooing their welcome,
And on her face, happy anticipation.
One dreary day of grizzling grey, I stopped
To greet and thank her for the simple beauty
Of her sweet endeavour, so often lifting
My spirits, when sorrow had sapped my energy.
Her words came with much effort and struggle,
A result of the severe stroke she had suffered;

And I, in turn, saluted her courage,
The gift of love she brings to others.
Curious, I learned my lady of mystery
Had come from the Philippines to Britain,
Had served as a nurse in our N.H.S.,
For more than three dedicated decades.
And now, I chirped, you continue to serve
Your eager flock of feathered friends.
Her story touched my heart, at a moment
When xenophobic, racist remarks
Had surfaced from a stagnant well
Of bitter, frustrated discontent,
Two months on, from the muddied waters
Of the nasty, malicious Brexit campaign.
Later that night, a memory was triggered
Of a half-forgotten hospital visit
To an elderly friend. Look, she had whispered,
At the sad lady in the opposite bed,
Look, carefully, at the nurse by her side,
An oriental, Philippino, I guess,
See how he sits, spooning the food to her mouth,
Patient and attentive to her distress,
Only when that man is on duty,
Is that dying woman properly fed.
At other times, she lies motionless,

Left to fend for herself, til the food,
Cold-untouchable, is whisked off her tray.
My eyes, startled, signalled disbelief,
As my friend, senior-disgruntled, retorted,
I know what I'm saying, I see it every day!
A decade on, from that scene recollected,
My mind turned to the possible connection,
Based on a curious coalescence
Of stories and coincidences,
For my new friend, the lady of the park
Had told me her husband had been a nurse,
A very good one, she proudly declared,
But, sadly, he left this earth too soon;
And I miss him more than words can tell.
Then, once again, I remembered how
My elderly, hospitalised friend
Had opined, with unusual force,
He may be Philippino, not one of us,
But he is a tender, exceptional nurse,
In fact, a deal better than some of ours;
And gazing at his quiet, departing form
I had ventured, politely, to add, surely
An immigrant can become one of us!?
Well, I suppose you may be right, came her response;
Now don't get on your hobby-horse, I know

Exactly what you're going to say:
Without the services of immigrants
Our N.H.S. wouldn't last a single day.
We laughed, I squeezed my friend's slender hand,
You've taken the words right out of my mouth!
In a complex, multicultural world,
Should not compassion and caritas
Count for more, than the provenance of birth?

ONE OF US

5th September 2016

for Margaret.

Newcastle, 1950s and early 1970s,
Port Harcourt, early 1970s

The story spread, bushfire fast, a compound
Combustible, of multiple strands
Speeding down expanding gossip trails,
Each teller at pains to convey the drama,
With raucous laughter, disbelief, anger,
Congratulatory enthusiasm
Or outrage, at the bold effrontery
Of one woman's unforgettable,
Irrepressible, spontaneous eruption.
But what kind of woman, from oyinbo[1.] land
Had caused so many restless tongues to wag?

When news came of her father's decease,
She had left her husband, son and daughter
To return, for a while, to the land of her birth,
The tough north-east of industrial England
With its fast declining shipbuilding industry,
That had once brought the man she married,
As an engineering student

From the Niger Delta, Nigeria,
To Newcastle, in Northumberland,
So surface-different, from the home
They had, over the years, made together
In oil-troubled, turbulent, Port Harcourt City.

On her flight back, she smiled at the trick
She would play, arriving home, a few days
Earlier than expected, after his messages
That should she not make haste to return
After her necessary extended sojourn,
He might be tempted, in sheer frustration,
To indulge in a makeshift, shallow liaison,
For no Nigerian, in love with his wife,
Takes kindly to her excessive absence.
Don't you bloody dare, she had laughingly retorted,
Or you'll bloody well have me to deal with!
She planned to arrive back in the house,
While he would still be at work in his office.
The children, boarding in secondary school
Would later, giggle and laugh, at the tale
Of their Mother's sweet-surprise return.
First she would shower, then take the wrapper
He had given her, before her departure,
Wind and tuck the cloth around her,
Then slip, sleepy, under the bedcover,

An unannounced, fragrant surprise
Waiting to enfold him, tender in her arms.

The airport was sultry-dense with frenetic bustle,
As she haggled, ritually determined
To hold her own, with the taxi driver
Firmly informed, she was no ignorant
Oyinbo, newly arrived on African soil,
To be grossly decashed for a ride in his cab.
Please understand, young man, I'm a wife,
A mother, a tired traveller, simply
Anxious to get home as fast as I can,
So treat me, as you would your own sweet mother,
I am not the spoilt wife of some oil executive.
He laughed, I hear you Mama, and shook his head,
I no go make wahala² to spoil your journey's end!
As she moved to put her key in the lock,
Oroma rushed to her side, confused, surprised.
Madam, we didn't expect you back so soon.
God be thanked for your safe return.
How is your Mama coping with her loss?
I have been praying for both of you in church.
How was your journey, you must be hungry,
I think there's okro soup in the kitchen,
Is there anything else I can get for you?
She looked, direct, at the agitated lass,

Were there hidden secrets, was something amiss?
Oroma's words of welcome sounded awkward,
A tumbling cascade of concealed confusion.
She went upstairs, Oroma carried her case
Still strangely hesitant, ill-at-ease.
Throwing open the door, she kicked off her shoes,
Sending Oroma to prepare soothing tea,
As fatigue took hold of every limb,
And she stretched for a moment on the bed.

Then anger forced her onto her feet.
Throwing back the bedcover, a perfume
Unfamiliar, invaded her senses,
And on the sheet, covering the mattress
Lay tell-tale stains of illicit encounters.
For a moment, an image from the past,
Overwhelming, assailed her vision,
As once again, she stood before
The homesick student of yesteryear,
Asleep on the bus, weary, dejected,
Afraid to meet his landlady's cold demand
For rent unpaid, because his allowance
From home had, as usual, been delayed.
There he sat, disorientated, lost,
A young man, adrift, in an unfeeling world.
There she stood, a bus conductress, strong,

On occasion, sharp of tongue, wondering
How she would feel, so far from home, under
Louring Northern skies, instead of African sun.
Yes, she sighed, that was how it had all begun.
Now, she was the one, disorientated, lost,
The taste of homecoming, bitter in her mouth.
The taxi driver, cheeky, teasing
Had given no trouble, no wahala,
While, at home, trouble lay undercover,
Biding its time, waiting to ambush her.

Action, she thought, speaks louder than words,
So without more ado, she called Oroma again,
Forget the tea, there's a job to be done.
First, the mattress left the bed, stripped bare,
Carried with Oroma's help downstairs,
Then into the open, out of the house.
No, she ordered, not in the backyard,
Let him see its remains, as soon as he arrives.
I will teach him a lesson he won't forget.
Now bring kerosene and matches from inside.
Soon smoke drifted upwards, as the mattress burned,
Its acrid odour, at one with her rage,
A strange sight for neighbours and passers-by
To ponder, scratching their heads, wondering why;
And if anyone is bold enough to ask, she mused,

I'll say, justice must be seen to be done
And leave the rest to their imagination.
She went inside and took pen to paper.
I have gone to spend the night with a friend.
When you have restored the marital bed,
Come and beg forgiveness for your offence.
Don't think, because I am a woman
Of the working class, I won't defend
My honour, good name and self-respect.
This is my right and I have taken it.
Oroma, tearful, was instructed,
Give this letter to Oga[3], when he appears.
Suddenly, Oroma hugged her tight,
Sorry, I could not stop Oga bringing
To your bed, his woman of the night.
Never mind, for what you couldn't help,
You can never be blamed; but right now
She answered, my main concern, is applying
Corrective medicine to the man I still love.
Oroma replied, you be like one woman
From my village, strong, fearless;
I think you no be Oyinbo, but one of us,
An African woman, with the wrong skin colour.
Please don't pack and leave Oga for good.
He should be proud to have a wife like you!

<u>NOTE</u> – oyinbo[1] land- country of the white man

wahala[2]- Pidgin English meaning trouble. The Niger Delta is home to a multiplicity of cultures and languages. Traditionally, Pidgin English served as a means of communication for the purpose of commercial exchange and interaction between the Peoples of the Niger Delta and Europeans, its vocabulary drawing on both indigenous and foreign languages.

Oga[3]- term used to address a man of superior social status, marking differentials in class and wealth, can be roughly translated in English by the word "sir." However, the word "oga" can, on occasion, carry a humorous, even ironic connotation, the idea of a "big man", who thinks too much of himself, thus appearing rather "small" to others, from an ethical and spiritual point of view.

HABITS

10th December 2011

for Gennaro, Neapolitan incomparable!

The young man glances briefly at his watch,
Giving voice to his sense of lingering loss;
"It's nine in the evening, the phone will not ring,
I'm wrapped in the sound of silence again."
His listener-teacher, a woman
Of older, seasoned vintage,
Pauses, then responds in warm, gentle tones:
"For you, that hour sounds regret every day,
A reminder of painful absence,
At the end of a long love affair.
For me, it is the memory of children
Grown into manhood, now continents away;
But for us both, is it not clear
That love has the power
To delight, wound and heal;
And memories, salvaged from seasons of storm,
Can insulate the heart and still keep us warm."

I WISH YOU LOVE

4th April 2015

For Esther and James on the eve of their wedding.

I wish you love that charts a course, constant
In the fitful times of an inconstant world,
A light that burns bright on a summer's day,
Alive in the dark, when winter holds sway,
A place of safety, a shoulder to cry on,
Where joy, renewed, can of a sudden
Fly you to skies, in explosive delight,
Nourishing hungry bodies-and-minds.
Marriage is an intrepid adventure,
An exploration of the belovèd,
Through changing seasons of shared endeavour.
So I wish you love, with strength to stay the course
In the tsunami times of our troubled earth,
A beacon, undimmed, amid winter's gales,
A luminous light, on sweet summer days,
And, in the future, a full treasure chest,
Packed with memories, for your unborn heirs.

ORGASM

3rd December 2011

for Pauline and George.

It is fireworks exploding across the sky;
It is riding rapids and getting high;
It is surfing the shoreline, on the crest of waves,
Receding and returning again and again;
It is the throb pulsating from the dawn of time,
Connecting past and present and future lives.

A WOMAN'S PLACE

for Haroun Al-Rashid Adamu.

It is said, my sister
That Hauwa's husband
Cannot stand the shame
Of her recent promotion
In salary and fame,
That when she softly suggested
He manage the home,
From Monday to Friday,
While she was far away
Battling to build a brand new
Girls' secondary school
In her home state,
He thundered, defensive,
That national development
Was no mandate for
Anarchic wives to abandon
Husbands, children, family and friends,
Indulge in devious games and wicked ends,
Lose all sense of decency and modesty
And dare to defy man's god-given authority.

Demurely determined, she replied
That her mandate came from
The ministerial mouth of a man
Devoted to his country and Islam.
To refuse to comply, co-operate, try
Would signal disobedience and disregard
For one, whose faith impelled him
To wage, Educational Jihad[1.]
Against those who mangle and mutilate
The words of the Quran and Prophet,
Imprison wives in ignorance
And sentence daughters
To premature marriage beds,
When their tender lives
Are still fragile – unripe.

Her husband's sharp words
Of ill-tempered anger,
Rebuffed Hauwa's efforts,
At carefully reasoned,
Diplomatic persuasion:
"It is not my job to return from work,
Supervise the maid in the kitchen
And the children with their homework,
After my wife has thrown open the door
And invited demons of chaos and confusion

To feed from my table, usurp my control!"
These words were crafted and designed
To underline his total rejection
Of Hauwa's stubborn commitment
To deviate from acquiescence
And quiet submission to his
Authority and expectations.

When his vitriol and threats fell on deaf ears
And Hauwa refused to yield to his pleas,
He carefully calculated a sweet revenge
And without more ado, he pulled out
The polygyny card, from under his sleeve;
But Hauwa's friends had foreseen
Her impending plight and had
Prepared for this very fight.
No sooner was the innocent installed,
Than Hauwa's classmates and former colleagues
Called and called, again and again,
With relentless, endless, repetitious rounds
Of collective congratulations
And choruses of celebratory sounds.
They would enter his office
To enquire after the new bride,
Drive daily to his compound,
Silent censure in every smile,

Praise his choice of new bride,
Ask to bless the marriage bed
And, wordless, demand hospitality,
Long after his purse had been
Drained and relieved of its load.
The bride's modesty and poise
Were acclaimed, in a twittering
Hyperbole of animated voices,
From a flurry of fluttering feminine forms;
And, somehow, their sickly-sweet, siren songs
Sucked all the naira[2.] out of his hands,
While he dutifully danced to their tune,
Wondering how their witches' magic
Made so many banknotes fly
With such ease, to rest-imprisoned
In their eager, grasping fingertips,
Promises, of how they would personally
Escort his lovely new wife to the market,
Quickly made, ostensibly for his approval,
Since, sadly, Hauwa was not around
To help her select the latest,
Most elegant cloth[3.] in town;
And, almost every day, when he came
Home for well-earned rest and respite,
Their gossiping laughter would drive him wild.

Early in the morning, one of them would appear
To collect the bride and whisk her off
To dress and braid and adorn her hair,
At vast expense, he knew not where.
Silently, he cursed those demon well-wishers,
For though the wedding had been
A discreet ceremonial affair,
A man of substance, it was generally, agreed,
Must lavish and spend, to a certain degree,
On friends, hangers-on and his new family.
Yet cunning and cruel, those vultures invaded
Every nook and cranny of his wretched life,
Making the last crumpled naira,
Of his salary advance,
Grow wings, fly and fall
Into their predatory hands.

His friends began to remark
To one another, that their brother
Seemed ill at ease, irritable
And the senior accountant,
In his government department,
Complained that a new bride,
No matter how enticing-beautiful,
Was no excuse for late-coming,
Dozing or disgracing his profession.

Even his mother, worried, remarked
That his second wife, unlike the first,
Had an insatiable appetite
When it came to devouring
Her darling son's wealth,
And eventually concluded,
That the best solution
Was to tell the world,
She had come on trial basis,
Did not meet their expectations
And would soon be sent back
To her parents and family.

Exhausted, Hauwa's husband
Readily agreed, for his new bride
Had rudely threatened to reveal
He was too tired, tedious and old
To pay her the dues, her beauty deserved.
How could he face his new in-laws
With this public humiliation and worse?
But Hauwa, calmly, came to his aid,
Smoothed his furrowed brow,
Convinced him, there was a way
To restore his equanimity,
Peace and tranquillity:
"My dearest husband, father

To our five, fine, flourishing children,
Why the whole world knows
You are too wise and mature,
Too powerful, respected and proud
To allow a mere schoolgirl's
Charms, tantrums and tears,
To destabilize, a seasoned man,
Of your experience and years.
No money need flow back
To your new in-laws
And they will most likely praise
Your name, for evermore,
When we offer their daughter
A place in my school;
In this way, your name
And honour will be restored,
Your Mother's worries removed
And your unhappy-second-marriage,
Quietly, carefully, dissolved.
Perhaps, in the next long vacation
We might consider going on Haj[4.]
To Saudi Arabia, a sacred duty
Our wealth, carefully tended,
May, Inshallah[5.], allow us to realise;
And as an Alhaji[6.], your colleagues

Will give you, once more,

All the respect you are entitled to."

Once again, peace and love

Returned to their marriage bed,

For he saw Hauwa's loyalty,

Common sense and diplomacy

Had triumphed over his ill-advised

Misadventure, in misplaced revenge.

NOTE – Educational Jihad[1] -the Arabic word Jihad refers, <u>in general</u>, to the notion of struggle, in this case a struggle to improve educational opportunities and provide greater access to educational institutions. In Islamic theology there is a broad distinction between two types of struggle, namely, the Greater and the Lesser Jihad. The former refers to the struggle of the individual, to achieve self-improvement and high ethical standards, regarded as a lifelong undertaking and obligation. The latter, or Lesser Jihad, concerns the right to self-defence and the defence of family, property and land. The search for and acquisition of knowledge is obligatory for every Moslem man and woman. Hence, in this poem, Hauwa's response to the need for educational development in her home state can be viewed, from both secular and religious perspectives. I am grateful to Dr Sinan Al Rawi for explaining the difference between the Greater and Lesser forms of Jihad.

naira[2] -the Nigerian currency.

most elegant cloth[3] -material, local and foreign, ranging in quality and price, that is taken to a seamster or seamstress to be turned into fashionable attire.

Haj[4] -a pilgrimage to Mecca. Surplus wealth permitting, this is a duty and aspiration dear to Moslem hearts.

Inshallah[5] -God willing, if God allows.

Alhaji[6.] -a title given to one who has made the greater pilgrimage (on the 8th to 10th day of the 12th month) to Mecca. The title confers respect and status. (Alhaja is the female version).

GENERAL COMMENT – Stereotypes of Northern Nigerian women abound, both in Southern parts of the country and in Europe and the U.S.A., their continuing struggle against gender inequality, all too often ignored. That struggle takes many forms, as I discovered!

THE GRADUATE

for Safiya.

<u>Northern Nigeria</u>: Bauchi State 1970s; Zaria,
Kaduna State, late 1970s and 1980s

When her father refused her
Permission to attend secondary school,
She sold her favourite wrapper[1.]
To pay for the bus ride,
That took her far from
Relations and friends
Village and home,
Alone, unprotected, unaided
Save for the scholarship award,
Nestling moist in the safe
Secret hollow between her breasts.

When her husband refused her
Permission to sit for J.A.M.B.[2.],
She bit her lip, registered
In silence unobserved,
And wrote the last paper,
While her womb growled
Unwelcome warnings that
Her second baby might make

A first impromptu appearance
On the examination room floor.

When her husband ordered her
To stay at home and
Mind her children and house
Like a proper wife should,
She uttered no sound
Of reproach or complaint,
Just packed her bags,
Rented a room in Samaru[3],
And called for her Mother
To come and carry her baby,
While she joined her classmates
In crowded lecture rooms.

Her husband decided not
To repudiate his pretty wife,
Transferred to Zaria and lowered
The level of domestic strife.
When the clamour of their children
And his visiting nieces and nephews
Laid siege, subversive, to her studies,
She carried her books, stealthily
To the quarters at the back,
And resolutely prepared

Her long research essay
By kerosene lamp,
The maid from her village,
Loyal-supportive,
Sworn to secrecy.

Now her framed photograph
Hangs next to his,
Trophy to her tactful persistence;
In her graduation gown,
She smiles, modest and demure
Yet insistent, unashamedly sure
Of the success she has won
In her guerrillère campaign,
One long battle braved,
In a series, only just begun,
As she looks for a way
To send her young maid to school.

Out of the late harmattan[4.] chill,
Change, unexpected, is on its way.
On reflection, her husband's
Scowling misgivings transform
Into smiles of self-congratulation.
He is glad for having sensibly
Conceded, to his dear wife's

Doggèd determination,
To scale the walls
Of academic achievement,
For now, he can take
His sabbatical in the U.S.A.,
And leave her with the children,
To maintain the home, and pay
For her needs and theirs
From her salary alone.

NOTE – wrapper[1] -cloth, local and foreign, usually worn ankle length, tied in different ways according to gender and regional variations.

J.A.M.B.[2] -the Joint Admissions Matriculation Board on whose authority, admission to university depends.

Samaru[3] -a residential area of Zaria.

harmattan[4] -variant form of the Fanti word "haramata," meaning a dry parching land-wind, which blows during the months of December, January and February. Its presence can be all pervasive, coating everything with a red dust, even, at its most severe, obscuring the air. It is during this season that diseases such as meningitis can occur, all too often proving fatal in cases affecting very young children and infants.

THE EVIL THAT MEN DO, AND SOME GOOD TOO

11th September 2009

This poem in three parts is dedicated to deux médecins sans frontières, toujours courageux et exemplaires: Dr Izzeldin Abuelaish and Dr Pauline Cutting.

First Voice – Secular Jewish Businessman

Place – London

I care only for family and friends,
Politicians are self-serving shysters
On whose promises, none may depend,
Although, in retrospect, I cannot ignore
How John Bull was kind enough to unlock his door;
And admit my father, orphaned by a war
That industrial-ruthless would devour
Millions, scapegoated in genocidal jaws.
My history is the scarlet of uprooted lives,
Bequeathed down centuries of ancient strife.
The Children of Israel have suffered too long;
How can I, competitive-affluent in cynical London,
Blame them for seizing their place in the sun?
All I can say, all that I know,
Is that family and friends

Give me strength to endure,
In a world, torn apart,
Still bitter and blighted,
Forever insecure.

Second Voice – Exiled Iraqi Father

Place - London

I came to this country with hope in my heart,
Searching for ways to mend the broken pieces
Of shattered lives and make a fresh start;
But my son, volcanic with anger before
The winged death machines called "Shock-and-Awe,"
Blames me, for securing his safety
And transplanting his life, on alien soil.
He claims kin with other lost brothers
Banished from their ancestral land,
Packed like caged beasts, held fast
Under U.S.-Israeli lock and key,
In apartheid dispossession
The West pretends not to see.
He accuses me, with youthful disdain
Of heaping disgrace on the family name;
And has vowed through his deeds

To blot out the shame.

His Mother's pleas were politely refused,

When our son spoke of a higher cause,

Insisting God's word could not be ignored;

And that, come what may, soon

He would leave London's shores

To play his part in global wars

According to Islamic law

And wreak revenge, long overdue,

On crusading Christian and infidel Jew,

In a world, overwhelmed by tsunamis of woe,

Where high-tech attacks, on the helpless below,

Yield colossal casualties, swift and sure,

For those who created this Wild West show.

Now that he's gone, I'm bereft of a son.

All I can say, all I can do

Is look to what remains of family and friends,

Somehow survive and strive to endure

In a world worn weary and insecure.

Third Voice – Bereaved Palestinian Father

Place – Gaza

In Israel, rabbis, army-embedded,
Incited young men, to blast Gaza anew,
To "shock-and-awe" and brutally subdue
Those they had labelled, sub-human, non-Jew,
While compliant from his polished
White House pew, a President,
Rhetoric glossy and new,
Mouthed mild concern for
The slaughtered and slain,
Their deaths, soon cast aside,
Ignored and unnamed.
In concentration camp Gaza,
The rabbi-roused soldiers,
Immune to a father's impassioned plea,
Had, voracious, victimised
With cruel, calculating eyes,
The brave beauty of the widower's
Peace-loving Palestinian family.
Scarlet stains, imprinted on walls
By purposeful Israeli shells,
Tell of daughters, blasted
Innocent, from evening studies

Into the jaws of untimely death,
Caged songbirds, silenced,
Smashed beyond redress,
Their screams, swallowed
In the mortuary's abyss.

As Gaza's doctor laments his loss,
Adamant compassion in his voice,
Defiant, he refuses to disappear
Into the endless vortex of hate-and-fear.
How can I, who heal Moslem and Jew,
Allow the killers of my children
To kill the humanity in me too?
My darling dead daughters
Deserve so much more than
The brutalizing legacy of war.
I shall love my neighbour whether
Moslem, Christian or Jew,
For, if not, how could I continue
To honour what I hold
Eternal, sacred and true?

WAR IS PEACE

1st September 2009

In near-empty churches, vicars preach precaution,
Lest peace-promoting handshakes propagate infection,
Spreading death and disease, through pestilent pigs,
The latest pandemic to test all our wits,
While prayers offered for lost British lives
Spiral down from sad, offended skies.

Still choirs sing and thuribles swing
For regiments marching in patriotic charade,
Uniforms and flags on martial parade
To museum-cathedrals, where clerics,
Councillors, colonels and warmongers gather
To resurrect, unrepentant, cost what it may,
The imperial past, for another bloody day,
While smug prayers for lost British lives
Spiral down, like dead birds, from offended skies.

Vicars, ministers and pastors bless
The newage warriors of war-is-peace,
With yet another Judas' kiss,
And dispense mellifluous words of comfort
To bereaved British families,
Detained for life, in unanswered

Questions and unrelieved distress,

As guests and celebrants on Afghan soil

Are turned to corpses in nuptials of war.

Smug prayers offered for lost British lives,

Spiral down, like dead leaves from stricken skies,

While those in authority and power,

Arrogant, employ obfuscation,

Glibly offering a concoction

Of false-patriotic evasion,

Secretive silence, confusion or lies

To ordinary members of the Common People,

Demanding to know, for what righteous cause

Their nearest-and-dearest have given their lives.

NOTE – 1.) "War is Peace", one of the iconic phrases from George Orwell's futuristic novel "Nineteen Eighty Four," published in 1948 and written when the author was terminally ill with tuberculosis, is key to his understanding of the evolving rôles of state power, surveillance, propaganda and thought control.

Raymond Williams helps us understand both the limitations and relevance of the phrase and its significance in the novel as a whole:

> "As a comment on a perpetual and normalised STATE of war its details may be wrong but its feeling is right. 'We are the peace movement,' a British Government minister said recently (in 1984) supporting the next phase of rearmament."

Raymond Williams also links Orwell's concept of "DOU-BLETHINK" and its application, to the 1980's and early 1990's:

> "Thus it is an obvious case of DOUBLETHINK when the radical Right, now in power in so many countries, denounce the state at the level of social welfare and economic justice,

but reinforce and applaud the state at the level of patriotic militarism, uniform loyalty, and control over local democratic institutions."

SEE – Orwell. Raymond Williams. London: Fontana, 1991, pp.111. and 118.

I suggest key British and U.S. events of recent years fit into this deeply disturbing political paradigm.

2.) In 2009, in the wake of the H1N1 Virus, His Grace the then Archbishop of Canterbury (another learned Dr Williams) instructed clerics to tell their parishioners to temporarily desist from shaking hands, during the Sign of Peace, a ritual in Anglican church services.

HIS STORY, HER GREATER UNRECORDED GLORY

yet another poem, for yet another unsung
Nigerian heroine.

The General writes his memoir
About how the war was won,
Without footnote or tribute
To the wife who struggled on,
Against all odds, in dangerous exile
Where he had dispatched her
To feed his children, protect his parents
And keep the family one.

Centre-stage smart, he looks the part,
In his ceremonial uniform,
Swagger-stick tucked under his arm
And on his chest, a new addition to
The serried rows of polished medals,
Gleaming bright under African sun.
He is brief hero of the hour,
Blinded by the illusion of power.
The crowds applaud; his smile is broad,
As the nation, momentarily grateful,
Thank him for a job well done.

Before the President, his wife bends low
To hear him praise her husband, in dulcet-tones:
"A man you must be proud of,
Whom I can always rely on."
"Oh indeed, your Excellency, it is quite so,
For without him, what would we all do?"
"And don't forget," the Head of State adds,
"Not all wives are as lucky as you!"

COMMON WEALTH USURPED

for ALL the Peoples of the Niger Delta, trapped in both
an internal and external petroleum imperium.

There will ALWAYS be Ikwerre,
He pronounced, civil war hardened,
Drunk with oracular absolutism,
While I, guest on land raped toxic
By leaking pipe lines and air fouled
By futility of leaping gas flares,
Spoke only sceptical silence.
Can the earth and ancient creeks,
Raped and poison-impregnated,
Sustain the progeny of patriarchs
Profligate in procreation,
Choosing to avert their blinkered eyes
From the encroaching devastation
To be visited, uninvited,
On innocent, unborn lives?
Yet, stripped of hubris, we may begin
To refocus and recognize
That our own self-destructive
Species may not long survive.
Could it simply be the case
That the Earth Goddess, exhausted

By the greed of the "master" race,

Is about to impose her own

Long-awaited breathing space?

If man's lust for wealth and war games

Escalates, riotous-unrestrained,

Then our species will damn itself,

Futile-weary into extinction;

But, liberated from our fearful dispensation,

Planet Earth may, in time,

Recover and evolve,

Bringing new forms of life to birth,

Ensuring Ani[1] is once more honoured

And at last receives respect and love.

NOTE – Ani[1] – (also Ala, Ale, Ane), "the most powerful deity in the Igbo pantheon, for she was not only the owner of the soil but also the controller of morality and creativity, artistic and biological." Often depicted with a child on her left knee and a raised sword in her right hand, her essence exhibits duality "a telling juxtaposition of formidable (even implacable) power and gentleness."[1]

"She is mother and judge."[2]

SEE – [1] Morning Yet On Creation Day. Chinua Achebe. New York: Anchor Press/Doubleday, 1975, pp.33-34 and [2] The Education Of A British-Protected Child. Chinua Achebe. London: Penguin Books, 2009, pp.108-109.

STOLEN SEASON

13th December 2010

Sometimes, when in winter's thrall under snowy skies,
Warm memories still kindle bitter-sweet smiles.
My love was deep and fine and true;
But in your hands, prized only when new,
The brief bauble of a frolicking fool.
Yet, had you been wisdom-blessed and honest too,
I would have stayed the course, to the edge of doom;
But you wove a web of lies around my soul,
From which I had to navigate my way home,
And take back the dignity you had stolen.
Two worlds, once joined, fell apart,
For one of the lovers had no heart.
Sometimes, when in winter's thrall, under snowy skies,
Warm memories still kindle bitter-sweet smiles.

SOUP ON A WINTER'S DAY

February 2010

in Canterbury.

A watery concoction
Of dubious origin
Has persuaded me,
For the moment
Hibernating at home,
Not quite discontented
But very much alone,
To pull out the large soup pot
From the back of the cupboard,
Roll up my sleeves
And get to work,
Conjuring the old magic
Of nourishing Scotch broth,
Vegetable thick
With a spicy kick,
Stock and barley enriched,
Satisfying-warm
To soothe, both heart
And faltering muscle and bone.

The phone rings as
The soup in my pot

Simmers and steams,

After a' that peeling,

Cleaning, chopping, cutting,

For a guid[1] Scotch broth

Is lang[2] in the making,

Preparation lengthy, followed

By slow, patient cooking.

So after a blether[3]

Wi' my Sassenach[4] Friend,

Laced with my words

Of boastful self-congratulation,

I invite her to come

The following day

And share the contents that

Will fill my soup tureen,

Wi'[5] fare tae[6] satisfy

First Minister, student,

Builder, office worker,

Barmaid or the Queen hersel'.

Weel[7], my friend, cheeky, replies,

You've made me feel sae[8] hungry

I'll just pop roon[9] richt thenoo[10],

If that's awricht[11] wi' you?

And whar[12] didye learn

Tae speak Lallan Scots[13],

Fir I ken[14.] you're a bonny[15.]

Wee[16.] Sassenach lassie[17.],

In surprise, I quickly retort?

Och[18.], it's a guid number o' years ago;

But once, I had a boisterous boyfriend,

Wha[19.] spoke a strang[20.] Glaswegian patter,

Sae learnin' it, I simply had tae.

At this oor[21.] mouths were filled wi' laughter.

Such simple pleasures and exchanges

Can, on occasion, keep the gloom

Of wintry weather safely at bay;

And in the process, produce magic

To brighten up the dullest day.

Sae tae the wifie[22.], wha gied us a'[23.]

The best broth, for a dreigh[24.] winter's nicht[25.],

Let us drink a dram[26.] and bethankit[27.],

But first we'll tak[28.] a bowl of that soup

Tae keep us strang, cheerfu'[29.] and healthy!

NOTE – The words listed below are common in Scots varieties of English, and being half-Scot/half-Sassenach, they meandered, quite naturally, into a poem in praise of Scotch broth!

guid[1.] -good, lang[2.] -long,

blether[3.] -informal chatter, friendly and light-hearted,

Sassenach[4.] -the name given by the Gaelic inhabitants of Great Britain and Ireland to their 'Saxon' or English neighbours.

wi'[5.] -with, tae[6.] -to,

weel[7] -well, sae[8] -so, roon[9] -round,

richt thenoo[10] -right now, awricht[11] -all right,

whar did ye[12] -where did you,

Lallan Scots[13] -Lowland Scots,

Fir I ken[14] -For I know,

bonny[15] -comely, plump and pleasing,

wee[16] -little, often used with an affectionate connotation. Here "wee" works as an adjective. In earlier usage it functioned as a noun, meaning a short time:

"Bide a wee, bide a wee; you southrons (English as distinct from Scottish men) are aye (always) in sic (such) a hurry." Sir Walter Scott (1771-1832).

lassie[17] -a girl, a young woman, a sweetheart,

Och[18] -oh, Wha[19] -who, strang[20] -strong,

oor[21] -our, wifie[22] -wife (diminutive form, sometimes with an affectionate, sometimes a rather patronizing connotation),

wha gied us a'[23] -who gave us all,

dreigh[24] -long, tedious, dreary, doleful,

nicht[25] -night, dram[26] -a small draught/measure of spirits, especially whisky.

bethankit[27] -as in "the Lord bethankit," God be thanked, e.g. said as grace after a meal.

tak[28] -take, cheerfu'[29] -cheerful.

THE POPULIST STRONGMAN IN THE KREMLIN

15th December 2010

Can one, trained and tutored
In the dismal arts of the K.G.B.,
Convince the public, by promoting
A Hollywood-superman image
On T.V. and media screens,
That he is no wolf in sheep's clothing,
But the custodian of liberty?
Like his friend from sunny Italy[1.],
He can, cheerfully, croon and croak his way
Through a popular ditty of yesterday,
Proof of his rebranding energy,
In an age of show-room celebrity.
This man of the people, also chooses to be
Formidable friend of the new oligarchy,
For he is a man of many parts,
As lesser players were doomed to find out!

NOTE – These lines were prompted by a recent clip of Vladimir Putin crooning and an older one of our bare-chested brave, riding on horseback, with a studied air of insouciant machismo, Marlboro man reborn on Russian soil (minus the cigarette). French friends inform me that Nicolas Sarkozy employed a similar advertising image, during his presidential campaign. Such images are directed at a certain perceived category of potential female voters and supporters, where appeal to image is everything, a case of style over substance, a flight from engagement with political debate, politics reduced to crafted public relations and salestalk.

his friend from sunny Italy[1] -Silvio Berlusconi, former Prime Minister of Italy.

Closet Critic Versus Soldat Engagé

For Bradley Manning[1].

Part One

Sleek and smart with a toss of her head,
The U.S. scholar casually said
That her country's films on war-torn Iraq
Lacked gravitas, had fallen flat,
Because historical distance
Is a sine qua non[2], in order that
High aesthetic can truly be shown.
May I, a wordsmith for troubled times,
Invite her to sample the exposé of lies
By a young man, incarcerated back home,
For revealing, to the world,
The horrors of an imperial war
And the felt reality of "shock-and-awe":
Babes broken on a civilian killing field,
Innocents being smashed to corpses,
By madmen from high-tech machines
No Pentagon general ever wanted us to see.

Let us honour this young soldier of twenty three,

For daring to defend democracy

And disown the fascist warrior creed,

That incriminates children,

Blasted, abandoned and left to bleed,

Once curtly consigned to the untermensch[3.] breed.

Here is gravitas of the highest order,

A refusal to play conquistador,

Break down the door and steal the oil

Of those he was instructed

To trample on and ignore.

No, cries a voice, unflinching and direct,

Now buried deep, within the U.S.

Military-industrial-complex,

Those I am asked to label "the other"

I have shown to the world

As my sisters and brothers,

My sons and daughters,

My fathers and mothers.

Where Art Meets Life

for Felix Greene.

Part Two

May I remind our elegant
Erudite, U.S. superstar,
That at the height of an earlier war,
The unembedded Felix Greene,
Bravely, brought the realities
Of young Vietnamese patriots
To life, through his art
On uncensored cinema screens;
And although this war ended
Thirty Five years ago,
Deformity and pain are still inflicted
On blameless babes in the womb[4],
Leaving their mothers to cope with new woes,
Unleashed by culprits, long ago,
Whom they will never meet, or see, or know.

Art For Life In Times Of Strife

lines in homage to Pablo Picasso's "Guernica", or rather
the tapestry replica on prominent display in U.N.
headquarters, New York[5].

Part Three

Between great art and life, there can be no void,

Except where lies are left to breed undisturbed,

If not, why was the tapestry of Guernica

Covered and quickly hidden from view,

So that a general-turned-politician could

Smile before flashing camera crews,

As calmly, on cue, he proceeded to spew

Bellicose propaganda

For a war, that would yield

Disaster after disaster,

In patterns of destruction

He seemed eager to renew?

The Art Of Words That Need To Be Heard

For Muhammad Ali, another champion of endangered
democracy.

Part Four

Remembering one, who would not deliver
Public endorsement, for a far flung war
He could only denounce and abhor,
In words stark and unequivocal:
"No Vietcong ever called me nigger,"
I wonder if, martial man, Colin Powell
Has acquired the humility or grace
To look fascism's fury in the face,
And acknowledge, after
Due deliberation,
That no Iraqi citizen
Was guilty of attacking
His war-obsessed nation.
The power of words can, in a trice,
Slash through forests of fetid lies,
And, in a flash of truth-telling,
Illuminate the darkest of times:
He said, "No Vietcong ever called me nigger,"
Words of steely precision, we all remember,

For those "mots justes" delivered a knock-out-blow,

With pugnacious grace, in the heat of war,

Six words that echoed round the world,

Courageous, direct, daring, risky,

Bearing the weight of a cruel history,

Conveyed with the elegance

Of distilled simplicity.

No Vietnamese ever called Ali "nigger,"

Just as no Iraqi ever

Attacked the World Trade Centre.

Surely, art is most potent and alive

When it exposes war salesmen's toxic lies?

NOTE – Bradley Manning[1] -The U.S. soldier "accused of passing thousands of secret diplomatic cables to Wikileaks," had spent 254 days in a maximum security prison in Quantico, Virginia, by 7th February 2010. As a result of his treatment, or rather mistreatment, his current mental state (i.e. in February 2010) was described as "catatonic," after more than seven months in solitary confinement. According to one of the few people allowed to see Private Manning, he had "pallid eyes, suffers from exhaustion and is in a weak physical state… His only exercise is walking in circles for an hour each day in an empty room. He is not allowed to exercise in his cell and will be forced to stop if he attempts exercise. He is illuminated at night so that the guards can see him. Whenever he leaves his cell, he is in chains that encompass his hands, waist and feet." There is growing concern "that U.S. officials are pressurising him into confessing an association" with the Wikileaks founder, Julian Assange. The U.S. Government was alleged to be applying "selective pressure on Manning in efforts to get him to make a confession – be it fake or otherwise – against Assange." Clive Stafford Smith, director of Reprieve said that "holding him (Manning) in secrecy is utterly pointless and merely reflects a political judgement." The lawyer added "if the British were principled they would intervene."

SEE... "Health of soldier in Wikileaks case is wrecked, claim friends." Alexei Mostous. The Times. 7th February, 2011, p.18.

In the final weeks of Barack Obama's second term as U.S. President, he issued an Executive Order, authorizing Chelsea (formerly Bradley) Manning's release from prison in May 2017. Clive Stafford Smith's comment, with regard to the British factor in this case, reminds us of Chelsea's dual nationality: her mother is a Welsh citizen and British subject, her father a U.S. national.

sine qua non[2.] -somebody or something indispensable, absolutely necessary or essential.

untermensch[3.] -German compound noun, "unter" meaning below, under, plus "mensch" meaning human being, person. The English equivalent of the compound noun is "thug" or "gangster"; but I have used the word with the literal meaning of less than human i.e. dehumanized, given the status of subhuman.

blameless babes in the womb[4.] - Monsanto "with its genetically modified seeds" was "welcomed back" into the country by the Vietnamese Government in 2010. "Monsanto was one of the manufacturers of Agent Orange, which gave Vietnam its own chemical Hiroshima. In 2009, the U.S. Supreme Court rejected an appeal by lawyers acting for more than three million Vietnamese deformed by Agent Orange. One of the judges, Clarence Thomas, once worked as a corporate lawyer for Monsanto." In 1978 the last C-130s dumped "a quantity of toxic chemicals amounting to six pounds per head of (the Vietnamese) population," causing a "foetal catastrophe," according to information presented to the U.S. senate, a state of affairs which in John Pilger's words "made village after village a murder scene."

SEE – "The right you never surrender," John Pilger. New Statesman. 6th December 2010, pp.24-27.

Pablo Picasso's "Guernica"[5]. -In 1937, the Luftwaffe's devastating attack on Gernika was declared "a total success: surgically precise, and in its calculated effect on terrorizing civilians, just what had been hoped for," by the commander of the Condor Legion, Lieutenant Wolfram Von Richthofen. It is clear where Donald Rumsfeld and his fellow "Neo-Cons" (New Conservatives) found the blueprint for their "Shock and Awe" strategy, sixty six years later.

Simon Schama explains the idea that inspired Picasso's painting of the 1937 atrocity:

"the painting would have to speak equally to other barbarities past and future – to work through a symbolic language that could be universal."

In February 2003, before U.S. Secretary of State, Colin Powell held a press conference in the corridor of the U.N. Council Room, on military intervention in Iraq, the tapestry reproduction of "Guernica" was covered.

On 11th March 2004, 3 bombs detonated in Madrid, killing 192 civilians and wounding 2050. Across from the station, thousands "made their way over the road to 'Guernica' and stood before its pall of smoke and mutilated humanity."

SEE – The Power Of Art. Simon Schama. London: Bodley Head, 2009, pp.374-5 and p.395.

LEST WE FORGET

20th January 2014

(Recalling lessons from history, on the eve of the fifty
billion dollar Sochi Winter Olympics)

The pressure cooker exploded,
The Bolsheviks had arrived;
Remember how War followed War,
And how we thought Czardom
Had finally been swept aside;
Remember the Treaty of Versailles;
Remember the Wall Street Crash;
Remember the crushing humiliation
And the desperate poverty, visited
On hard-working German people,
Industrious and proud, like us;
And lest we forget, should it not be said
That their lust for imperial power
Was not so very different from ours?
Remember the Siege of Leningrad,
The living-dead, brave, on every street;
Remember the Gulag network,
Where cruelty was the régime,
And after the Fall of the U.S.S.R.,
The Vultures, descending from the West,

Eager to swoop and seize what they could,

Heaping scorn on us, while we endured

A storm of chaos and contempt.

So don't be surprised, as we rise again,

If our Leaders have turned tyrannical,

Exulting in the incendiary game

Of resurgent, fascist nationalism,

That blankets us all in euphoria and shame,

Hiding lurking fears, we are frightened to name;

And the only way to change direction

Is to break free, from the senseless system

That transforms victims, into brutal predators

Chasing revenge down centuries of pain,

Leaving new generations of widows

And orphans to howl and rail,

In the wind and the rain,

Groping and searching, amid the débris,

For ways to put the fragments

Of lives, carelessly shattered,

Back together, once again.

So let us resolve, with history in mind,

To break the paradigm, brutal, entrenched

In crazed, calamitous contests,

That can destroy with wanton haste,

What has taken centuries to create.

DIALOGUE

3rd December 2011

Between a reluctant English language student
and his teacher.
For Angelo.

"I'd rewrite history, if I had my way,

So that Italian would still be

The world's lingua franca today,"

My would-be N.A.T.O. Roman warrior declared.

"No need then to learn English phrasal verbs

Or struggle with the sounds of ugly, awkward words."

"But think, for a moment," came my reply,

"How many millions of slaves would have to die,

Constructing palaces for emperors and princes

Or sweat in coal mines, oil fields and ditches

To seize and rape Earth's resources and riches,

Or suffer slow crucifixion,

For guerrilla insurrection,

In endless lines, along the Appian Way,

Erected, gruesome, for public display,

Their tortured presence, like the Strange Fruit

Hanging, bloody, from Alabama trees,

Left to rot, by power-drunk,

State-sanctioned terrorists?"

"Well," came his quick-fire rejoinder,
"Do you think the story
Is so very different today?"
"Only if we remain in thrall
To the stale, pernicious pattern
Of imperial diktat and sway,"
And pausing for a moment, I went on to say,
"Think of Gandhi, Martin Luther King,
Nyerere, Mandela and Che.
Year by year, month by month, day by day,
The struggle, daunting, difficult, continues
An inescapable part of our destiny,
Just what being human is meant to be."
"So you say," he responded with a sigh,
"But now back to those English modal verbs,
The cause of my tribulation and woes!"
"Nil desperandum," I firmly advised,
"Your present efforts and martial determination,
Will, I am sure, bring you victory
In next month's examinations;
And please nota bene,
Let me make it quite clear,
That Latin and Italian
Abound in English vocabulary,
Though certain phonetic adaptations

May resemble mutilations,
To proud, patriotic Italian ears;
And as a European, not a nasty
Chauvinistic little Englander,
I love the treasured architecture
And art, of your great cities,
The rural beauty of your countryside,
The music of Vivaldi, Correlli,
Verdi and Puccini, the gourmet
Delights of your wine, pasta and pizza,
The Tales of Boccaccio, the Poetry of Dante...
Are not these enriching world exports
To be preferred, to the record, barbaric,
Of reductive-destructive
Imperialist aggression;
But what of the attitudes, stubborn,
Lingering in your Northern League's
Dangerous, divisive agenda,
Perhaps, you would care to speak
On this topic, in your English class, tomorrow?"
His answer came, with a mock salute,
"Yes my captain, I'll do my best;
And when I return to Rome, I'll be sure
To inform my superior senior officers,
Your language course, with cultural studies,

Made me feel I was on military training,
Not the semi-holiday I had been expecting!"

<u>CODA</u>: <u>Impasse</u>
An élite, drunk on poisonous nostalgia
For a past, based on imperial power,
Is incapable of making the transition
To a sober pursuit of policies,
Based on sound principle and reason,
In the interests of the Common People.

<u>IN CONCLUSION</u>
This, I told my student the following day,
Is the problem facing too many countries today,
Trapped in ill-fitting propaganda and lies,
Afflicting BOTH your country and mine,
Virulent-alive in the bellicose moves
And rhetoric of the U.S., Russia and China.
"There is much in what you say," he quipped,
"But I'm more concerned with real-politic;
And as an Italian, who wants to serve N.A.T.O.,
I made my choice, some time ago;
I prefer to serve Uncle Sam[1], than
The sons and grandsons of Uncle Jo[2]."
All I could say, by way of reply,

Is that we all must try harder

To bring into being, democracies

That work, in the interests of the Common People,

Whether European, North or South American,

Chinese, Indian, Pakistani,

Middle Eastern, African or Russian…

For our history, to-date, is a catalogue

Of conflicts, man-made, lurching

Unsustainable, towards Armageddon.

NOTE – Uncle Sam[1] -probably a humorous expansion of U.S., a personification of the United States of America, 1813.

Uncle Jo[2] -an ironic adaptation of the above, to refer to Joseph Vissarionovich Djugashvili (1879-1953), better known in the West, by his sobriquet or nickname, Stalin, meaning man of steel.

THE DARK INSIDE THE LIGHT

5th January 2010

written on the day Dubai celebrated playing host to
the tallest tower in the world.

The tower thrusts into the sky,
An illuminated rocket
Tethered to its base,
Tapering mountainous high
Named after the Caliph
Of petro-dollar smiles.
Who rode to the rescue
Of debt-ridden Dubai.
Flashing cameras and microphones
Could not record the faces of men,
Whose stories and struggles
Would never be told,
In the garish gaiety
Of a celebrity world,
Grains of stricken sand
Driven by desert storm,
Back to far-flung lands
And fond, fragile homes,
Men, whose names remain unknown,
Whose hands laboured for pittance pay

To bring architects' dreams

From computer screen into light of day.

This new tower, like the pyramids of yore,

Is luxury for the few, rising from

The toil of the industrious poor.

NOTE – 1.) "I stood on a hill and I saw the Old approaching, but it came in as the New…" Parade of the Old New. <u>Bertolt Brecht Poems, Part Three</u> 1938-1956. John Willett and Ralph Manheim editors, with the co-operation of Erich Friel. London: Eyre Methuen, 1976, p.323.

2.) "Why are the public buildings so high. How come you don't know? Why that's because the spirits of the public are so low." <u>Twelve Songs</u>. W. H. Auden. London: Faber and Faber, 1966, p.191.

OLD LIES IN MODERN GUISE or
PYRAMIDS ANCIENT AND MODERN

Warming to his theme with patriotic pride,
The Egyptian archaeologist declares
To the reporters, clustering eager at his side,
That the skulls and bones, disinterred, on display,
Represent more than the scattered
Fragments of long-forgotten lives,
Lying near towering pyramid
Of ancient pharaonic line;
For they provide evidence, convincing and clear,
That no slave labour was ever put to work here.
I wish I could have been there to ask
How much those men were paid
For completing the task;
And how their hasty burial rites outside,
Compared with the obsequies of a pharaoh
Whose death palace, they had
Struggled and sweated to provide.
Yet, lest we lose sight of the here-and-now
This questioner, stubborn, would like to know
Are the descendants of those nameless poor
Better served than their forefathers were?
Or are they still, exploited and insecure,

Rendered invisible, unworthy of interview,

Denied a place or space

In print or on screen,

Unremarked faces in crowds

Quickly passed by and never seen?

Yet, all that they are

And all they have been,

Creates the comfort-and-wealth

That rises like pyramids

To new heights obscene,

For every contemporary corporate-king

And conniving, acquisitive celebrity-queen.

NOTE – After writing this poem, I realised it was partly inspired by Bertolt Brecht's poem "Questions From A Worker Who Reads," written during his first period of exile 1934-1936, that is some 75 years ago, a poem I had not visited for over 2 decades. The fragment of television news, which prompted my response in poetry, also triggered memories of Brecht's impact on the Nigerian students I taught in the early 1980s, for the mark of great writing is that it is, both particular and universal, historical and timeless.

"Who built Thebes of the seven gates?
In the books you will find the names of kings.
Did the kings haul up the lumps of rock?
And Babylon, many times demolished
Who raised it up so many times?..."

SEE - Bertolt Brecht Poems, Part Two 1929-1938. John Willett and Ralph Manheim editors, with the co-operation of Erich Friel. London: Eyre Methuen, 1976, pp.252-253.

ANCESTRAL VOICES

The queen rides, serene, in her golden coach,
Sprinkling stardust, on her subjects enthralled,
Bestowing smiles on excited tourist folk,
While on dark streets, the homeless sleep rough,
As patriots, enraptured, soar in song,
Spell-bound, inside a royal concert-hall,
Exhorting an ancient, weary god
To ensure salvation, for those at the top,
Church and state in a gilded embrace
With City billionaires and global magnates;
And so a fairytale of feudal birth,
Confuses, distracts with cruel purpose,
The multitudes, sidelined by those they serve,
In our increasingly unequal world;
And surely the time is long overdue
To ensure the many, no longer
Live stunted, defiled, cyber-serf lives,
Bonded to the sick, insatiable greed
Of self-appointed lords of sub-humankind,
For creativity and liberty
Must walk hand in hand
To bring peace and integrity

To broken, war-weary lands;
And in that hour, the infernal tower
Of privilege-built-on-poverty,
To universal acclaim, will tumble down,
As the seeds of Thirteen Eighty One
Revive in fertile soil, to flower again,
And Blake's vision of a fairer Britain
Becomes Common Purpose and endeavour,
Sustained by the threatened achievements
Of a self-taught miner from Tredegar
And all the women and men of an era,
Defined by the Spirit-of-Forty-Five,
A spirit we are called upon to revive,
For Wat Tyler, Johanna Ferrers,
John Ball, William Blake, Aneurin Bevan,
And countless, uncounted heroic figures,
Lived and died for a simple, shining dream,
That a life, enriching, fulfilling
Become the inalienable birthright,
Gifted to every British citizen;
And this, of all dreams, inspires and compels,
Across cruel countries and down centuries,
A threat to every pirate-executive,
Profiteering from the labour
Of the world's disinherited;

And still, those ancestral voices can be heard,
Amid the cacophony of our distressed world,
We played our part, now you must play yours;
But hurry, for time may be running out,
As a myriad life forms fade fast from our planet,
Extinction threatening human survival
As monster-men extend their stranglehold,
Power-drunk tyrants, out of control,
Playing with death-toys, no nation should own,
In games of misrule and toxic growth.
The queen waves, serene, from her golden coach,
Performing her duties, as she was taught,
All too often, hobnobbing, uneasy,
With unsavoury rulers of suspect worth,
According to the selective military-
Commercial interests of the day,
Masquerades of hypocrisy,
No woman or man, regardless of rank,
Should ever be required to perform.
In this age of corporate hegemony,
We, the People, are disgraced and diminished,
Mere consumer-addicts, made blind to the process
Dismantling our Rights, from under our noses,
Yet still, those Ancestral Voices, anxious, murmur,
Intent on arousing us, from our stupor,

We played our part, now you must play yours;

But hurry, for time is running out

And democracy, wounded must not

Be abandoned to traitors, or left to die.

NOTE – 1.) The opening line of our official national anthem, frequently sends me, smiling, to Lord Byron's cheeky comment:
> "'God save the King!' It is a large economy
> In God to save the like;"

SEE - The Vision Of Judgement, XIII. George Gordon Byron. The Complete Poetical Works of Lord Byron. Boston: Houghton Mifflin Company, 1905, p.286.

2.) "Who will not sing God save the king
> Shall hang as high's the steeple;
> But while we sing God save the king
> We'll ne'er forget the People!"

SEE - Does Haughty Gaul Invasion Threat. Robert Burns. Selected Burns For Young Readers. New Lanark: Geddes and Grosset Ltd, 1996, pp.168-169.

3.) "It is well enough that people of the nation do not understand our banking and monetary system, for if they did, I believe there would be a revolution before tomorrow morning." Henry Ford (1863-1947), on the link between secrecy and excessive, morally suspect wealth accumulation/expropriation.

4.) "He who dies rich dies disgraced." Andrew Carnegie (1835-1919).

STORMDRIVEN

25th December 2016

Teachers, doctors, nurses and other skilled workers
Are packing their bags, fleeing the land,
Because their professions and institutions
Are falling prey to the greed, rapacious,
Of privileged profiteers' stranglehold,
Government and corporate interests,
Brazen-contemptuous, trampling
On the dwindling rights of the Common People.
Private has devoured public,
Competition, ruthless, prized over
Kinder, gentler co-operation,
Success, a matter of grab-what-you-can,
Poverty, accelerating all the time,
The rich, skilled-superlative-slick
At expensive, legal tax evasion tricks;
And in this ethos of feverish misery,
How many mainland Europeans
Would now choose to come and work in Britain,
To fill the expanding skills' deficit
In a fast-imploding, polarised system?
University professors wring their hands,
As more British students pack their bags,

Seeking ways to ease the mounting pressure
On the stressed savings of Mummy-and-Daddy,
While mainland European academics
Turn their backs on British campuses,
Sensing a chill in the air and shrinking horizons.
If this exodus gathers momentum,
The queen may soon stand, lonely on her balcony,
Wondering why even the tourist trade
Seems in decline, perhaps overpriced
Pomp and pageantry dulling to shabby,
Wondering, what has happened to her nation,
Wondering why there's no-one left to wave at,
Wondering, what on earth has happened
To that brave, post-war consensus,
Ushering in the Welfare-State-Renaissance.

It was the People, not the empire brigands,
Who moved that Dream closer to realisation.
Will their children, grand-and-great grandchildren,
Passive, permit wholesale destruction
Of a priceless heritage, being stolen from them?
Surely, the Spirit-of-Nineteen-Forty-Five
Is needed now, a reminder, powerful,
Of what a certain momentum can achieve
When Common Good takes centre-stage?

In our bleak-confusing times, let It
Come home from temporary exile
To feed hungry hearts, inspire active minds.
Now is the time to turn the tide
And reclaim, what by stealth and guile,
Has long been stolen from the common purse,
This a more creditable way, to honour
The unsung heroes of a besieged Welfare State,
Than merely playing a part, passive-docile,
Colluding in suspect, idle ceremonial.
In the interests of a United Queendom,
I would petition her most gracious Majesty
To employ the Royal Prerogative
And help end this parlous state
Of unhappy, contentious discontent.
When successive governments fail the People
To whom, should they, in extremity turn
Save the Royal Mother of a distressed nation?
But should the Lady be worn out, exhausted,
Let the People's voices prepare the way
For democratic, peaceful, consensual
Constitutional change, a process
That could, at last, bring into being
An exemplary, written Constitution
That enshrines fundamental human rights,

To which every citizen can have recourse,
A giant, rainbow-coloured umbrella,
Offering shelter, justice, protection,
In our fractious, storm-driven times,
Manipulated by cabals of liars.
Now, there is need, urgent, to turn the tide
So that the People's voices can be heard,
And the Ship of State change direction,
Averting imminent shipwreck
On jagged rocks, threatening
National disintegration.

In Nineteen-Forty-Five, not so very long ago,
Citizens of a war-weary, bankrupt Britain
Had the vision, the determination
To work, undeterred, for the Common Good,
In the face of privileged opposition.
Surely in Twenty-Seventeen, we must
Look again at what they achieved,
The obstacles overcome, the mistakes that were made.
To honour those efforts, Gargantuan,
Of tenacious women and men,
Should we not roll up our sleeves, work together
To retrieve and safeguard the treasures
Their labours of love created,
Entrusted, bequeathed to us?

In time present, time past and future conjoin,
So many connections interwoven,
In a tapestry, demanding, requiring
Careful, considered understanding.
Hasn't the time come, when short-term
Myopic politicians should not be entrusted
With the fate of peoples, countries, continents
And nature's ravaged, depleted resources?
When the People's voices and needs are ignored,
When the centre, crumbling, cannot hold,
The ghosts of fascism will threaten return,
Sneaking, casual, through the backdoor,
Promising prosperity, begetting
More conflict, suffering and war,
As wild-empty promises disappear
Vanishing, ephemeral, into thin air.

The sands of time are slipping through our fingers
The Ship of State must change direction,
And in order that the tide will turn,
The People's voices must be heard,
Clear, alert, informed and honourable,
With leaders, schooled to listen and learn,
In a climate, that values
Wisdom over ostentation,
Honesty, unsullied by the crude insolence

Of pervasive public relations industries,
Integrity, ascendant over lies,
Intimidation and bribery.
If this be simply, too much to ask,
We, surely, forfeit our right to live on Earth
On the magnificent planet, we have failed to love?
The time is now, the moment has come
When we must, belatedly, civilize ourselves
Or be forced, abruptly off the stage,
Storm-driven into oblivion,
Consigned like dinosaurs, to a bygone age,
As the planet, exhausted, heaves sighs of relief.
The sands of time are slipping through our fingers
And remedies, vital, need concerted action.
Can our capacity for mindless destruction
Be converted into sustained programmes
Of sensitive, co-operative reconstruction?
Can we make ourselves worthy of the planet
We have raped, despoiled and failed to care for?
Can we evolve, beyond our continuing
Capacity for sadistic, lawless cruelty?

NOTE – After sharing these lines with a friend, she expressed the view that in the county of Kent where I live, many would find the republican undertones I have given voice to, unpalatable, unacceptable. All the more reason for their presence, came my rejoinder.

Later, I recalled George Orwell's prefacing remark at the beginning of "Animal Farm:"

"If liberty is to mean anything at all, it is the right to tell people what they don't want to hear."

Given the inroads privatisation has been making into tertiary education, an increasing number of British students have moved to mainland European countries for undergraduate and postgraduate studies. Brexit is likely to curtail this phenomenon and hence further reduce the options available to British students. Recently, there have been reports in the media of an increase in the number of female students, selling sexual services to older men, so as to cover their basic living expenses.

With fewer overseas students predicted to come and study in a less hospitable, more inward looking, prohibitively expensive D.Q. (Disunited Queendom), and a fall in the number of British students willing or able to take on prohibitive debt, our universities may suffer decline and loss of income, coming to resemble corporate businesses, catering for the children of the global one per cent, as institutions close their doors on those who merit places, but lack financial support. (Enter the Jude the Obscures of the twenty first century). British academics fear losing E.U. funding for research and the collaborative contribution of E.U. colleagues from the mainland, wary of moving to a less hospitable, more unpredictable environment.

One likely outcome is that Britain replaces a relatively more egalitarian European education system with the U.S. model, so that a dominant profit orientated private sector erodes, then displaces an underfunded failing public, or semi-public sector. Fundamentalist "free market" privatisation has already destroyed an integrated rail service, has been making rapid and significant inroads into our N.H.S., as well as school system and prisons. M.I.T. Emeritus Professor Noam Chomsky describes the road to privatisation succinctly:

"Defund, make sure things don't work, people get angry, you hand it over to private capital."

SEE – Stewart-Lee's article on the dangers of privatisation affecting the N.H.S. The Observer. The New Review. 14th February, 2016, p.7.

But, the demise of our besieged Welfare State is still not inevitable if we, the Common People, look to our history and defend what our parents and grandparents struggled to create for us and our children. Indeed, in reviving the Spirit-of-Nineteen-Forty-Five, should we not share it with others and our despairing cousins on the other side of "The Pond," priced out of decent education, health care, housing, transport and employment?

More than seven decades ago, Eleanor Roosevelt argued the case for creating a National Health Service in the United (?) States! In 2017, the U.S. President and his Wall Street cronies are bent on rescinding the modest reforms to a prohibitively expensive private health care system introduced by his predecessor.

During the 2016 U.S. election, senator Bernie Sanders voiced support for something far more radical than "ObamaCare," namely the introduction of a publicly funded U.S. National Health Service.

A post-Brexit-Britain is likely to fling open more doors to U.S. corporate health care (?) companies, in effect, sounding the death-knell for OUR N.H.S., but doubtless a scenario that would be greeted with p.r.-packaged jubilation by the U.S.-Anglo-one-per-cent, gleefully pursuing their profiteering agendas!

Some years ago Dr Adetoun Ilumoka, passed on to me, advice given to her by a Chinese friend:

Hold fast to dreams,
For if dreams die,
Life is a broken-winged bird
That cannot fly.

FOOD FOR THOUGHT or
LOUISE'S BROWNIES TO THE RESCUE

December 2011

The words I needed, to fashion my song,

Eluded my grasp, like leaves on the run,

So facing defeat, I switched the kettle on,

Seeking solace in a mug of piping hot tea

And Louise's mouthwatering, tempting brownie.

Chocolate mellow, moist and buttery,

It melted my frustration, like ice in the sun,

As I took up my pen, determined to go on

And finish the task I had earlier begun.

Soon, helter-skelter, words flew, fast and thick,

For me to appraise and take my pick,

Conjured by the culinary magic

Of that brownie's scrumptious intercession,

Transporting the eater from Hades to Elysium.

LA BONNE MÈRE NOËL

December 2014

for Louise again.

Louise, m'a complètement accablée
De sa prodigieuse générosité,
Tout simplement, La Bonne Mère Noël,
Créatrice d'une fête, exquise et belle.
Elle dépose son sac lourd de largesses,
Gonflé de plats, divers et riches,
Amassés exprès, pour chaser les nuages
De mon humeur, mélancholique et tenace;
Et qu'est-ce que je puisse l'offrir de ma part,
Sinon des simples remerciements sincères
De m'avoir rendue le goût de l'espoir,
Car son cadeau de Bonheur m'est arrivé
Tout inattendu, dans une saison de malheur,
Doucement offert, pour que je sorte,
Peu à peu, de l'enfer hivernel,
Qui m'est entouré d'une source lointaine,
Médicament supérieur
D'une bonne Mère Noël.

PETALS OF LOVE, PART 1

6th November 2015

for Rose S.

Dark descended dreigh[1.], while chilly fingers
Wrapped a shawl of ice around my soul,
As on that day, remembrance of things past
Lingered uninvited, determined to stay,
Predicaments, present, laughing in my face,
Thoughts rotating, restless, out of control,
As rain, wind-driven, lashed the window panes
And sullen street lamps flickered, then failed.
The knock on the door came urgent and loud,
Caught me unawares, startled by the sound.
Cautious, I peered into the cheerless street;
And there she stood, a bouquet of roses
In her outstretched hands, splashes of yellow,
Petals of love, shielded from wet assault
Of anarchic cars and playful gusts
Of untamed winds, running amuck.
"No," she replied, "I won't come inside,
Must get home, retrace my steps,
Nearly lost my way in the dark,
Thanks to the absence of light on your road;
But I was determined to give you

These flowers, today, a little sunshine
On a chilly, windy, rainy birthday."
A year later, in a cosy café,
Into my arms came another bouquet,
Roses, yellow-bright, to take home with me,
Friendship expressed in a gift of beauty.

NOTE – dreigh[1] – lowland Scots, meaning wet, dull, gloomy, dismal. Standard British English has no single word to convey the combined effects of dour weather on a dull, dreary day!

FIVE POEMS FOR THE KIDNAPPED VICTIMS OF BOKO HARAM

CHRISTMAS 2014

12th December 2014

Number one

the first in a sequence of 5 poems for the 276 Chibok
schoolgirls kidnapped by Boko Haram and the women
and girls in their thousands, they subsequently abducted
and enslaved, who have received much less publicity.

The miracle we seek each Christmastide
Is an end to the cruelty plaguing mankind,
For the child in the crib, we come to adore,
Lies trapped in our worship of futile war,
As Earth cries out in deepening distress
At the cold lust of men, intent on conquest,
High-tech careless of the harm they unleash,
Deaf to the pleas of the child in the manger
Pleading, in vain, for an end to this terror.
How then should we sing of Peace on Earth,
While killer drones fly lethal above,
And children, at school, are dispatched premature,
In a pitiless maelstrom, out of control?

THE PRESENCE OF ABSENCE

14th April 2015

Number Two

for the remaining two hundred and nineteen enslaved
Chibok schoolgirls and the Disappeared on every
continent of planet Earth.

Their purpose camouflaged in the dark,

Burst, volcanic, into demented fury,

Plucking the stars out of young female eyes

In explosions of futile male cruelty,

Ripping hope out of innocent hearts

Assaulted with envious impunity,

By men, posing as holy warriors,

Mere slaves to demonic depravity.

Soon families shed tears of stunned disbelief

At the failure of generals, eminent,

Strangely silent, verbose politicians,

And their cheerfully uncharitable wives,

To value the lives of Chibok daughters,

Snatched from their school, their education,

Their very future disappeared into slavery,

Driven deep into a forest of despair,

Minds and bodies, coerced and concealed

In the dull shrouds, we saw them compelled to wear.

Now a year has passed, some would have us believe
The Chibok-Abandoned-Disappeared
Will remain, with regret, forever lost;
But women of good faith, across the earth,
Do not accept collusion with the curse
Of patriarchal tyranny at loose.
No religion, cult or political system
Should be allowed to cripple the potential
Of women and girls, on the basis of gender,
For tyrants are, of necessity, enslaved
By the very slavery their tyranny entails,
Nor can token women in privileged positions,
Adopting cosmetic masks and public smiles,
Effect the changes that will ensure
The safe return of every Chibok girl
To family, friends and unimpeded access
To educational opportunity and work success;
And men who cling, compulsive to power,
Content to disappear and destroy
Growing numbers of their sisters and brothers
Will forever peer, insecure, over their shoulder,
Fearful of an assassin's lurking shadow,
Or a predator drone, unleashing its venom.
As for the fanatics of Boko Haram,
The Nigerian oligarch, plutocrat

And cunning, conniving kleptocrat,
Like his counterpart, the whole world over,
Is content to see the poor, the struggling
And dispossessed squabble in murderous
Mayhem and confusion amongst themselves,
While he protects his ill-gotten gains
In gated mansions and distant tax havens;
But, above all, foot soldier of Boko Haram[1]
So long as you, pitiless, oppress your sister and brother
You will poison your soul, a zealot in the service
Of your corrupt, mafia-style masters,
Perpetually stunted, imprisoned
In the chains of carnage and cruelty,
Deaf and blind to the lessons of history;
And though a long year of frustration has passed
Since the nightmare theft of precious young female lives,
Their absence is present in global hearts and minds,
Car nous sommes toutes les étudiantes de Chibok;
And their present plight is a blight on our world;
Et puisque les chansons de ces oiseaux
Précieuses-enchaînées sont réduites
Au silence dans un tombeau bouché,
Pour les dernières lignes de ce longue poème,
Je chante, je répète le célèbre refrain,
Nous sommes toutes les étudiantes de Chibok,

Aujourd'hui et demain, jusqu'à l'heure inconnue

De leur libération, exigée

D'une patience, tendre et tenace,

When we will sing and celebrate and dance

To those three sweet, sacred words: free at last!

NOTE – With reference to the "foot soldier(s) of Boko Haram" (Western book learning is forbidden), may I refer the reader to the words of three wisemen:

> (i) "People are never more dangerous than when they have nothing left to believe in except God." J. G. Ballard
>
> (ii) "I believe that a world free of fervent religious belief would be a safer place for everybody." Sir John Mortimer
>
> (iii) "If Africa falls to the will of the fanatic, then the insecurity of the world should be accepted as its future and permanent condition." Professor Wole Soyinka

SEE – Of Africa. Wole Soyinka. New Haven and London: Yale University Press, 2012, p.130.

In West and Central Africa, the calamitous impact of Boko Haram and Daesh affiliates, in many ways mirrors the depredations and suffering unleashed by the L.R.A. (Lord's Resistance Army) in Uganda and neighbouring East African countries, the former in the name of Islam, the latter in the name of Christianity.

DOUBLE JEOPARDY I

Number Three

"When a country is in crisis (often) one of the first
things to go is rights for women," Alexandra Kollontai.

The cruelty of Boko Haram,

Blights the innocent wombs of girls

Spurned and unloved in an unkind world,

Unable to celebrate a rare return

When villagers turn cold, hostile eyes

On one of their own, with Boko Haram inside.

Better she had died, than inflict a curse

On family and friends, with that belly

Carrying abomination not blessing.

But, surely, if Amina and her child

Have the right to renew and shape new lives,

They need, all, that loving care can provide,

For why should the innocent be locked again

In prisons of suffering only death can end,

Rejected, as human refuse, by foe and friend?

There is no homecoming for Amina

And her sisters, unwilling bearers of new life,

    Because village patriarchs,

Along with Boko Haram,
See women as commodities
And the property of man.

DOUBLE JEOPARDY II

28th September 2015

Number Four

The answer partly lies in a lesson from yesteryear.

So what do we do when our wives and girls
Return home, damaged beyond repair,
Bearing progeny we cannot claim as our own?

And you, what right have you to outlaw and condemn
Your women, will you violate them again,
Instead of stemming the flow of their tears
And welcoming them back into your hearts and beds?

Here is a stalemate, ancient and modern,
Embedded in the history of war
Across millennia and continents,
Yet, surely, there must be a kinder solution,
Than provoking fearful young women
Into self-imposed exile, or untimely graves,
Fleeing from hardship unrelieved,
In a bitter season of stress-without-end?

Then, of a sudden, I remembered
The stern-kind words of an Ikwerre captain,
In the closing agonies of war's catastrophes,

Commanding fathers, brothers and husbands

To cherish the young girls and women

Rape and death had failed to take from them,

    For surely it is better to heal

    What has been injured but not broken,

    Than engender a lethal legacy

    Of bitter self-hate and destruction.

NOTE – As second-in-command to the Military Administrator of Port Harcourt, Captain Elechi Amadi was ordered by Colonel Adekunle, commonly referred to as "the black scorpion," to bring the city back to life "within a month," after it had been retaken by Nigerian federal forces, in the closing stages of the Biafran/Nigerian Civil War (1967-1970).

On one occasion, he was faced with the helpless fury of men, whose women and girls had been abducted from a refugee camp, to which they had subsequently returned, after having been raped. On the day immediately prior to these events, Captain Amadi had personally assured those in the camp of their security. Filled "with a sense of failure and desperation," he loses his temper. A dose of verbal shock therapy ensues, with brutal harshness:

"'Now listen, all of you,' I said. 'My main concern is to find you food and shelter and to protect your lives. If you have not realised by now that this is an all-out war in which anything can happen, then you are fools. Women you have been raped; so what? All you need is hot water'...

'and you men, aren't you happy that you have your wives and children with you, naked and hungry though they are? I am not as lucky as you are. My wife and six children, my parents, brothers and sisters vanished two years ago. I am not talking of rape; I am talking of death.'

A hush fell. The men were tongue-tied and ashamed. Some of the women began to sob in sympathy. My short speech worked like magic, and there was not a murmur of complaint thereafter. I thought this self-pity made my work easy and cheap, and I made up my mind never to mention my personal sorrows again."

SEE – <u>Sunset In Biafra</u>. Elechi Amadi. London: Heinemann Educational Books, 1973, p.151 and pp.174-178.

POWER AND IMPOTENCE

14th August 2016

Number Five

In the skirmish between vigilantes
And deranged, self-appointed tyrants,
I took my chance, slipping desperate
Through the net, running, resting, hiding,
A shadow, stealing furtive-determined
Out of the forest, away from my captors,
Choosing to risk disastrous collision
With the madmen of my misery,
Than remain slave to their depravity,
Preferring to embrace the bridegroom Death,
In act of defiant finality,
Than submit to the daily-nocturnal
Assault on my womanhood, my humanity.

Exhausted-triumphant, I knocked on the door
Of my father's house, collapsing into
The welcome of my mother's enfolding arms;
But happiness proved a malevolent mirage
To one carrying Boko Haram inside.
She has brought disgrace, is a curse on us all
Were the whispered words of disapproval,

Circulating, poisonous from home to home,
Following my uncertain steps, at every turn.
Then, one night, I heard my father speaking
In low, guarded tones, to the wife at his side,
For all our sakes, it were better she had died.
My tears ran their course, though I stifled my cries.
For me there was no home, no place to hide,
No future, for the child, in the land of my birth.

I have decided to return to the zealots in the forest,
I will choose martyrdom, pretend compliance
With conversion, miraculous, to their cause;
And after training, I will make of my body
A deadly weapon of war; but my target
Victims will be of my choosing, not theirs,
For I will discharge my suicide belt
In their midst, so that my unborn child
May be protected from entering
The hell they have made,
On the earth they have cursed;
And before I leave my father's house,
A shadow, stealing furtive-determined,
Back to the forest camp of my captors,
I will leave a farewell note for my family,
Informing them, I will never allow
The babe in my womb to enter a cursed,

Corrupt-cruel, inhospitable world;
And the gods, worshipped in mosque-and-church,
In the blighted village of my birth
Would surely disown the harvest of death,
The incendiary conflict, waged in their names,
Raging in a nation, where the poorest
Are despised, neglected, rejected,
A nation raped, looted, divided,
Unworthy to receive the baby I carry,
The baby for whom, death will come as a blessing,
Spared the starvation and suffering
I saw, etched on the faces and bodies
Of the innocents in my father's village.
Though I have no home, no place to hide,
I seek my husband Death, with head unbowed.

CODA – Forms of Slavery

Why do tyrants fail to understand
That love thrives not in the clutch of cowards' hands,
Since both master and slave are confined brutally
In a noman's land of blighted sterility?
Only when man renounces the imperial urge
Will he free himself and learn to love,
No longer trapped in the conflagrations
Born from his lust for domination.

When rural poverty is neglected,

In states, stagnating on the periphery

Of an oil-exporting-dependent

Economy, do not be surprised

If zealots and fanatics

Rush in to fill the void,

Promising power, wealth and recognition

To despairing young men, they train as killers,

With the promise of creating

A new theocratic empire

And an assured place of privilege,

In an exclusive, imperial heaven.

When one tyranny seeks to replace another,

The harvest can only yield

More terror and suffering.

NOTE – Four years ago, Professor Wole Soyinka opined:
"If Africa falls to the will of the fanatic, then the insecurity of the world should be accepted as its future and permanent condition."

Out of Africa. Wole Soyinka. New Haven and London: Yale University Press, 2012, p.130.

Is it not also axiomatic, that if men the world over continue in their perverse attempt to colonize, exploit, abuse and control women, global insecurity and misery will certainly persist?

Ironically, in so many African cultures, to rephrase an old Chinese saying, women hold up more than half the sky as farmers, traders, mothers, musicians, doctors, poets, scientists, teachers, nurses, civic and community leaders, peace-makers, technicians... Why then are so many men, so cruel-afraid of them?

MOVING ON

24th February 2013

She once loved the man she thought he was,
For a while, his presentation was unsurpassed;
But when she peered behind the mask,
She knew the time had come to get out fast,
Lest he shatter her into fragments.
Of wilfully scattered shards of glass,
For men who play dishonest games
Are usually found out in the end;
And trust, once broken, is hard to mend.

The trouble, she mused, with men of his breed
Stems from the imperative of power
Domination, self-doubt and greed
And the simple failure to understand
That love cannot be locked in a cage,
Where its song will subside into dumb outrage,
Its beauty destroyed, its lustre dimmed.
Love is not stolen loot, stashed in a safe,
But tender passion, born of mutual respect,
Where minds sing in harmony, before bodies meet.

SEPARATION

2nd March 2013

He said, you no longer love me.
She replied, I will love forever
The man, for a while, you chose to be,
In that brief, brilliant time when you were
Beautiful in thought, word and deed,
A stallion, dancing amid the stars,
Leaping and plunging, cavorting and free,
Asking me to join you in our space odyssey;
But, of a sudden, you seemed bent on retreat,
Afraid of where this adventure might lead,
Frightened to cast aside the presumptuous pride,
That reared in a frenzy, blotting out the light,
Trampling and annihilating
What, once, you had dared to desire,
All too soon killing love
In a wild lust for power.

LOVE IGNITED

21st December 2013

I knew I could no more resist such love
Than a mother ignore the cry of her new born,
Or swallows refuse to heed the call
That carries them far from winter's thrall,
Or oceans cease their timeless ebb and flow,
Or raging storms their destructive roar;
And so my head spoke sternly to my heart:
This rose bears thorns, lacerating-sharp,
For such love, once ignited, can blaze and burn,
With power to heal and power to harm,
Creating voyages to unknown worlds,
A searing force that enraptures and wounds.

AFTERMATH

4th March 2014

The treachery of Civil War
Shipwrecked his humanity
On a desolate shore,
Nor would he ever trust again
The motives of his fellow men;
And the pain, locked within his stricken soul,
Impelled him to wound the women
He lacked the courage to love;
And the children he fathered
Found him, distant and cold,
A patriarch, slave to the fear
He might lose a suspect-control,
Disguising human frailty
In the proud officialdom of public rôles,
Deploying practised wit and worldly charm,
To mask a sense of isolation forlorn,
For the wounds of war are landmines in the soul,
And casualty-survivors of uncivil strife,
Once disowned and betrayed by
Boyhood classmates, neighbours, friends,
Often rush headlong to exact revenge,
Blind to the harm they inflict on themselves.

The casualties of war include, unrecorded,
The silent survivors, as well as the dead.

THE DREAM LIVES

24th December 2015

I am a moment in a winter wind
A fleeting second in the summer sun,
Carrying a dream as old as time,
Precious and fresh, like a life new born;
And though you took a dagger to my heart,
In the dismal urge to conquer and control,
Enslaved to the oldest imperial curse,
The dream survives your wounding thrust,
Stronger by far, than the doomed assault
To seize it entire and cut it out,
For love is the hope of the whole human race
And woman must reclaim her usurped space,
Teaching man to abandon addictive war games,
Restoring him whole, in her healing embrace.

MEMORY

23rd July 2016

for Elechi and the Lady of Lake Oguta.

He is no more, and yet his haunting,
Sporadic, over decades and unshed tears,
Suddenly insists, insinuates its presence
Uninvited, in restless vintage dreams,
Joy and lacerating pain, unleashed,
An ambush of the senses, bitter-sweet,
Memories provocative, conflicting,
Resurfacing, unfaded, from the deep.

You emanated magic and mystery
The day we set off on that long drive,
You, seductive, teasing-flirtatious,
Playing sly-stubborn-cryptic,
Hinting, casual, at meetings with
Powerful water spirits of the deep,
For a while you and I, briefly intent
On escaping from the tangled web
Of local-global discontent,
Your eyes, sparkling, mischief-contagious,
Your need for solace in troubled times,
Part of the playful plot you had devised.

I drove, you directed, but where to and why?
Be patient, you replied, ask no questions
And leave this matter, in your lover's hands.
Soon the city ceded to countryside,
As I drove on, curious, in unfamiliar land.

The sun beamed brilliant on our mood and minds.
I told you my surprise would yield delight,
You called out, with laughter in your eyes,
As Lake Oguta held us spellbound.
Her waters embraced us, we cavorted,
We swam, woman and man, at peace at one,
In moment serene, under Nigerian sun,
All divisions of misapprehension and history,
Suspended in elemental magic and mystery.
Your strength, your beauty overwhelmed me,
Your tenderness, gentle, as you held me,
Your words, embedded still in my memory:
You are my woman and always will be;
And my response, swift, tremulous:
It seems the Spirits of this luminous lake
Have power to heal, renew, remake,
For what we share, what we have in common
Makes a mockery of false divisions,
The crippling distortions of corrupt histories.
Our meeting is not only of woman and man,

But of Europe and Mother Africa,
Transcending past and present hurt,
Confirming the sacred promise of what
Human encounter could and should be;
You are the love of my life and always will be.

He is no more; and yet his haunting
Suddenly insists, insinuates its presence,
For though our paradise was lost, dishonoured,
The dream we shared, left an imprint strong;
And though we failed our dream, the Dream lives on;
The Water Spirits of Lake Oguta
Continue, generous in their welcome
And enshrine its sacred song,
For the roots of Mother Africa
Offer nourishment to everyone.

INVOCATION

25th July 2016

They say he was a prodigious-fruitful man,
How many seeds ripened under his sun,
Came her question, mischievous, provoking,
To which I had no convincing rejoinder,
So I replied, in light-hearted vein,
Enough for a football team I suspect;
And had you asked him the question direct,
He would doubtless have cited tradition,
As he did, on occasions when it suited him
To deploy words of selective pragmatism:
In Ikwerre, such enquiry amounts
To demeaning, impertinent interrogation,
All the more so, to one of chiefly status.
It is singularly unseemly, typically Oyinbo[1.]
To speak of human life in crude numbers,
As if one were counting goats or chickens,
Such a crass European way of thinking.
Perhaps his perspective was influenced
In part, by an anti-rational undercurrent
That family planning was an occidental plot
In a combative, neo-colonial world,
Yet who, I wondered, had sent him yearly,

New information on family planning?
Could it have been, a lady of spirit
Independent, bearing the brunt
Of that prodigious-fruitful energy,
Armed with Ani's empowering blessing?[2.]

Now that he waits on the other side,
Surrounded by ancestral spirits,
Comradely compañeros and old friends,
I wish to address the Goddess
Of Fertility and Justice, direct,
And lodge a redemptive, timely request.
For his next incarnation, let him come back
As fertile woman, strong of brain and heart
To experience to the full, childbirth,
Nurturing and child rearing, in accord with
The number of offspring, for whom he remained
All too often, an absent, distant stranger;
And in this way, he will learn to honour
Woman and cherish all Ani's children,
A long overdue, evolutionary step
In a humanizing direction.
I appeal to Ani, in the name
Of sacred, usurped, disrupted traditions,
Pre-dating false, misogynist takeovers
And disruptive colonial upheavals,

For a better world is impossible

Without gender equilibrium;

And though patriarchal power

Still proves a stubborn-resistant,

Pervasive omnipresence,

Across Earth's troubled continents,

The future depends, not on warrior men,

But on the rightful guardians of Earth's fertility,

So I lay my prayers, my plea, my request

At the feet of One who works to effect

That essential, restorative redress.

NOTE – Several decades ago, after Elechi had read a draft of my verse drama "Amina," (context: Northern Nigeria, subject: the struggle of women for greater access to formal education), he asked me whether I wished I had been born male. I replied no, because in patriarchal societies to address and resolve the inequities of gender imbalance and inequality of opportunity, it is women who must assume primary responsibility, though male support is important and to be welcomed. Then, and frequently over the years, I thought of some of the many inspirational African women, past and present, women unbowed, strong in their womanhood, their sense of civic duty, economic rôles and responsibilities and their bold initiatives, as catalysts for change. I thought of Kenya's Wangari Maathai, Egypt's Nawal El Saadawi, Somaliland's Edna Adan Ismail, Uganda's Betty Bigombe, Malawi's Chief Theresa Kachindamoto, Nigeria's Funmilayo Ransome Kuti and, as I am writing, the recent heroic struggle of Dr Ameyo Adadevoh to prevent the Ebola epidemic from spreading throughout Nigeria, a struggle in which her own life was endangered and for which, tragically, she paid the highest price, but a struggle that succeeded in achieving its vital objective.

During our many discussions about politics and society, I had commented that Ikwerre and Igbo women were luckier than their British counterparts, in having Ani as their pre-eminent, cultural deity. (For further information concerning Ani, see NOTE NO1. <u>Common Wealth Usurped</u>. p.117.) Were these lines to reach him now, on the Other Side, I can see laughter in his eyes, followed by the oft repeated comment:

"Nawao for this woman, wetin I go do with her self!"

The answer of course: to have liberated his love from the distortions of patriarchal imperatives.

And so I offer a challenge to his conflicted, restless spirit, soon to join the queue awaiting reincarnation.

Elechi was bilingual in Ikwerre and English, with an interest in the Yoruba and Hausa languages. After listening to me converse in French with visiting French officials to Port Harcourt, he was charmed by the beauty of that language and decided he would like to acquire some rudimentary skills in a second European language, with a strong presence on the African continent and began to learn basic French, so I offer my challenge in French, "car la lutte civilisateuse continue, une lutte sans fin, une lutte créatrice, parfois dure, toujours exigeante, qui engage, surtout, les esprits forts et courageux."

Let him return to play his, or, if my request to Ani bears fruit, HER part, in the necessary struggle to correct gender imbalance.

This is one of the continuing and vital challenges to which I often refer, invoking Ani as a guide and source of inspiration, because in her various manifestations, she is both the arbiter of justice and when necessary, the agent who administers and implements justice. She is the deity to whom all, regardless of sex and gender rôles, are required to defer. She remains a potent presence, animating institutions such as the Wives' Councils and the Umuada, the clan daughters, two complementary institutions, particularly important in Ikwerre and Igbo exogamous cultures. Ani's essence combines power and gentleness, artistic and biological creativity. She is the Guardian of morality, ensuring social cohesion and unity, with power over female fertility and the fertility of the soil. Thus, through her, the rôles of women, as mothers and farmers, procreators and food producers, are revered. Yet, at the same time and from a historical perspective, we see how colonial interventions and disruptions challenged the powers of the Goddess and female authority, as men often began to emphasize patriarchal privilege and prerogative over female authority. So, let this man return to his people as woman, in a process moving beyond past and present hurt, to more civilized, kinder encounters and engagement between women and their fathers, grandfathers, brothers, sons, friends, husbands and lovers. "C'est une lutte qui engage, surtout, les esprits forts et courageux," and Elechi's spirit was on many supremely challenging occasions, strong and courageous.

IN MEMORIAM

For the One who felt the beat of my heart,

But from whom, for my sanity,

My very survival, I had to depart;

And yet the leavetaking would

Remain forever incomplete,

For when love takes hold

With such strength, such depth,

Its roots remain alive to the end;

And beyond the finitude of our brief lives,

Our love is enshrined in our beautiful child.

The narrative, sketched in these simple lines,

Echoes the story of all humankind,

As love crosses borders, seeking

Consummation that will not be denied.

NOTE – "...Love is not love
   Which alters when it alteration finds..."

"...Love's not Time's fool, though rosy lips and cheeks
   Within his bending sickle's compass come;
   Love alters not with his brief hours and weeks,
   But bears it out even to the edge of doom..."

Sonnet CXVI
William Shakespeare

HOPE AND BETRAYAL,
BETRAYAL AND HOPE

7th August 2016

On that day of timeless, distilled joy,
The Water Goddess of Celtic lore
Seemed wordless-present, coalescing
With the radiant Lady of Lake Oguta,
Transforming us, spellbound-blessed in her waters,
Woman and Man, united in harmony,
Cultures and countries in equilibrium,
History transcended, borders vanishing
In sweet rebirth of Common Humanity,
Freed from the fetters of male aggression,
Man, at liberty to find love again,
Woman, revered in the strength of her giving;
But that day of timeless, distilled joy, dimmed
To a shadow, reproachful, of what might have been,
If you had summoned courage enough
To cherish and honour the gift of the Goddess,
All too soon, trapped, once more, in labyrinth
Of ruthless, conquistador imperatives,
Yet the Dream, elusive, continues
Its journey through time, an undercurrent
Waiting to resurface, resurrected

In the precious genes of unborn lives.

Thus, you and I are links, historical,

In the unfolding, disruptive, evolving

Drama of being, dying and becoming.

Out of the ashes, the phoenix takes flight,

Bidding her mate to do better this time,

For the Dream, though wounded, refuses to die.

NOTE – In a multiplicity of myths, across countries, cultures, continents and millennia, water is frequently present as:

> "a metaphor for love itself. Like water, love stayed with the man who held it loosely, as in an open cupped hand; but the man who tried to grip it hard in his fist, found that it flowed away and left him gripping nothing."

SEE – The Women's Encyclopedia of Myths and Secrets. Barbara G. Walker. New York: Harper Collins, 1983, p.1066.

STRIKE ACTION

for the wives and daughters of Aluu and Umueze.

Like dogs, fighting fanatic over juicy bone,
The Nwosu men, enraged, declared war
On their brothers of the Nwachukwu clan,
Over a strip of farmland,
Each claimed as their own.

The trade in abuse, insults, scurrilous words
Had escalated immoderate to poisonous proportions,
As the snakes' fangs were bared
And the crescendo of curses prefaced
The belligerent exchange of bruising blows.

From family patriarchs and male elders
Orders were abruptly issued and relayed
To certain members of the Wives' Council[1.]
And the Umuada[2.] without delay,
That Nwachukwu women were to cease forthwith
From all communication, conversation, co-operation
With Nwosu daughters, sisters, mothers and wives,
In a struggle that was now
Insidiously impinging on all their lives.

After months of dangerous discontent,
Bitter bickering, unresolved conflict,

Young Chide Nwosu was found dead at dawn,
His lifeblood carelessly spilled and spent,
Harvest of hate that could unlock
Fearful floodgates to frenzied feuding
And endless revenge killings, which would
Ravage the village, like a virulent virus,
At loose, on the run,
Pursuing the young, for generations to come.

The wives met in emergency session,
Deliberated at length and sent
An emissary to announce to the men
That by all that was sacred to Ani[3.]
They had come to issue their own ultimatum
And command their bellicose husbands and sons
To cease their acts of abomination at once.
As the President of the Women's Meeting
Proudly lifted her head,
Her eyes blazed, militant
With tidal wave anger and indignation,
Silencing her listeners with eloquent denunciation.

You men, tempers aflame,
Burning in feverish
Fires of anarchic aggression,
Have you forgotten, so soon,

The lawful limits of your
Patriarchal powers and prerogatives?
Your mothers and wives have mandated
Me to come today and speak in their name,
Remind you of our obligations and traditions,
And charge you with bitter blame,
For sacrificing our son to your wanton war game.
To you, men of the Nwachukwu line,
Chide Nwosu's death may be of scant concern;
But, for the members of our organisation,
Each must protect the interests of the rest.
Know then, that the untimely
Death of this son of the soil
Is mourned and lamented by us all.

Since our village was founded,
All wives, who come in our midst,
Must join our number,
Swear to honour the Earth Goddess and Virgin Mother,
Live in peace and respect each other.
Our council's strength is sustained
By the solidarity we seek to maintain,
Through our lives' cyclical
Seasons of joy and pain.
When we celebrate childbirth,
Compose new dances and songs

To express our unity of purpose
On farm, in marketplace and home,
We are enunciating the ancient law,
That in our community
No wife or mother is ever alone.
Even the Oyinbo[4] warriors with their sticks of fire
Had to be chastened and chastised,
And taught that the voices
Of our mothers and grandmothers
Were not to be dismissed or despised.[5]
But you are not the District Officers of Old,
So why do you choose, to flout and ignore
An ancient institution, whose principles
Serve not only the interests of women,
But maintain your world and ours
In delicate balance and essential equilibrium?
Therefore, you reckless sons and hothead husbands,
My message comes to cool your collective fever.
We require you to discuss together, agree and deliver,
To the anxiously awaiting Council of Women,
An undertaking, that this madness will end
And peace prevail among us again.
And, finally, we remind you
In the name of the ancient Goddess,
That we are all her children;

It is we who belong to this land,
To use it honourably as
Time and custom demand.
When caretakers turn rapists,
Plunderers and pillagers,
The wrath of Ani will descend
To wreak havoc on us all,
Until we beg for forgiveness
And desecrate her no more.

But stubborn in strife,
The men, heedless, continued
To fight fanatic, like dogs over a bone
Which, in the end, none would take home.
So, once more, impatient, the women sounded their gong
And, insistent, called their members to come
In haste, to ponder and plan their response.
At last, when consensus was achieved,
The women rose, with hope in their hearts,
Confident their strategy would work.

When the children, chattering cheerful,
Returned from school, they found
Their mothers' absence from home,
Prolonged, past the accustomed hour
When they would trek back from market or farm.

Later, when husbands and fathers
Returned from work in field or town,
They discovered, to their perplexed alarm,
That cooking pots lay idle, empty and cold,
As ominous silence hung heavy in the air,
No sign of wives and mothers anywhere.
Had some malevolent masquerade,
Mischief-intent, passed this way
To lure their women and babies away?
Meanwhile, hungry bellies grumbled and complained,
So the men and schoolchildren set to work
To prepare a meal, that would not cook itself.

Soon, news spread bushfire fast,
That an emissary, from a village, some miles away,
Had just arrived with urgent message to convey.
Although their mothers and wives were safe,
Hospitably sheltered and well fed,
They had sworn, by the Earth Goddess,
None would return to the chaos they had left,
For no man should senselessly seek to destroy
The unity they had long enjoyed,
Without inviting consequences, beyond his control.

Thus, they had agreed to boycott their men,
Until tempers cooled, the land issue resolved

And sanity free to hold sway
In male heads and hearts again.
The elders and patriarchs lost no time
In summoning brothers, to attend
The crisis meeting they quickly convened.
It took a ceremony of purification,
Where Nwosu and Nwachukwu men
Swore, by the spirits of their ancestors
And household gods, in sacred shrine,
Before priests and elders, that no more blood
Would be shed, over land they would share
To appease the enraged Goddess,
Whose anger was etched on the face
Of every husband, who felt disgraced
By the cold welcome of a comfortless home
And the endless round of domestic chores,
He was, unwilling, forced to take on.

But, before the strike action was called off
At last, and their wives and babes returned,
Bills, for the generous hospitality received,
Had to be promptly paid, in cash or kind.
This, the women, unanimous, had decreed,
Knowing how promises, made under pressure
If not fulfilled fast, to the letter,
Would be left to rot and slowly fester.
So, the men, reluctant, made pilgrimage

Of repentance and offered their best
Chickens, goats, yams and palm wine
In grudging gratitude to their hosts and kin.

And so among the women, calm-determined,
Consensus was quickly-easily reached,
Agreement, unanimous, once more achieved,
For the moment was ripe, had arrived
To return with their infants and babes
To marital homes, where husbands, chastened,
Longed, lonely-impatient for their presence.
The President of the Wives' Council,
Satisfied, smiling, congratulated
The Members for their sweet-tasting victory,
With words that brought laughter, rippling, leaping
Lightsome with infectious sunshine relief:
"Let us hope that these unruly he-goats
Have learned the lesson to respect
Their wives' powers and prerogatives.
But even those, who, stubborn-slow,
Still lack a good dose of sound common sense,
Will surely have felt the pinch direct,
To their injured pride and depleted pockets!"
Soon voices soared in spontaneous song,
Bodies swaying, carefree in motion,
A celebration, tender, of tension released,
One problem solved, peace and harmony restored.

NOTE – the Wives' Council[1] -In the traditional dual sex economies of Igbo and affiliated cultures "women ruled over women, while men ruled over men." One of the functions of the Wives' Councils, especially in exogamous societies, was to discipline errant husbands. In the lingering, neo-colonial, patriarchal structures of south-eastern Nigeria, men are all too frequently unwilling to respect ancient female powers and prerogatives, at which point Ani may well step in and lend a hand!

SEE – <u>Male Daughters, Female Husbands</u>. Gender And Sex In An African Society. Ifi Amadiume. London: Zed Books, 1987, pp.152-3 and pp.153-155.

the Umuada[2] -the formal organisation of patrilineal daughters who possess "strong powers in the place where they were born." (Amadiume, 1987, p.59). In Igbo and Ikwerre traditions, their prestige and sphere of influence can have major significance in determining the outcome of complex political issues in the communities, where they were born and grew up, even when marriage and/or work have taken them far from their natal homes. (Amadiume, 1987, pp.59-63).

Ani[3] -see explanatory note after <u>Common Wealth Usurped</u>, p.117.

Oyinbo[4] warriors -in this phrase, the Igbo word "Oyinbo," meaning white person or Caucasian, refers to British soldiers serving the frequently challenged interests of imperial hegemony, with weapons of destructive intensity, "their sticks of fire," i.e. firearms, including rifles and machine guns.

dismissed or despised[5] -In 1929, the women of south-eastern Nigeria went to war against the colonial government, over the issues of taxation and the system of Warrant Chiefs, instituted and imposed by the British. Ǫgu Umụnwanye (the Women's War) covered an area of some 520 sq. kms. and brought an end to the corrupt, hated Warrant Chieftanship System. This militancy typifies a long tradition of resistance to colonialism, on the part of both women and men, in many parts of the African continent.

SEE – <u>The Ibo People And The Europeans</u>. The Genesis Of A Relationship. Elizabeth Isichei. London: Faber and Faber, 1973, p.142. And

The Road To Aba. A Study Of British Administrative Policy In Eastern Nigeria. H. A. Gailey. London: University of London Press, 1971, pp.108-111.

IKWERRE MOTHER or MAMA ELECHI

for Chioma's paternal grandmother, who
"backed" her son to school, ensuring his
continuing access to formal education.

To complete primary school,
Her son must enrol
In a neighbouring village,
Some distance from home.
His father frustrated
Threw up his hands,
Helpless resignation
In his voice and words:
But the place is too far,
And I no get money
For transport, so what
In the name of Ala[1.]
Do you want me to do?
Ah, but what won't
An Ikwerre mother
Do for her only son?

When she came back
From her cassava farm
And prepared soup and foo-foo,
Her little son's silence

Cast a shadow over her heart,
Ah, but what could she do?

Some mornings later,
She came, late but elated,
Breathless and beaming,
To her cassava plantation.
One woman teased her,
Thinking she had spent
A late night and morning,
In her husband's arms.
Ah, but what won't
A Nigerian woman
Do for her only son?

And when the pattern persisted
For more than a week,
Her co-wives went as emissaries
To their husband's reception room,
Intent on tackling the problem
Their investigation had uncovered,
In words of crafted diplomacy
But challenging, to the point:
Our sister treks every morning,
Backing our son[2], when his legs,
Too weary, refuse to walk on.

All this, so that he can
Complete the remaining
Two years of primary school.
We have come to tell you
That this load is too much,
For one who must labour
On her farm and then return
To bring her son home,
At the end of his schoolday,
Now too long, too far away
For our tired sister and our son.
The women, careful in their
Consensus of subtle-damning
Criticism and condemnation,
Silenced their man, with the sting
Of shame, that threatened
To mock his manhood
And tarnish his name.
Ah, but let it be known
Across the nations of the world,
African woman can be
As cunning as the spirits,
As fierce as the lioness,
As daring as the eagle
And more devoted than

Any man, in steadfast
Devotion and service
To her belovèd only son.

The man summoned his wives and kin,
Smiling, confident, to his reception room,
And there, with fine-tuned
Chiefly decorum and dignity,
He cleared his throat and declared:
I have decided that our son
Will lodge with an aunt of mine,
So that he may complete
The two remaining years
Of primary school, and we will
Pay for this welcome hospitality,
In part, with food, palm wine,
Yam, cassava and okro from our farms.
The women nodded sage-approval:
Our husband has spoken well
And will do even better!
Ah, but when all is said and done,
What won't a mother do
To satisfy some of the dreams
And desires of her only son?

NOTE – Ala[1] -variant form of Ani, the Earth Goddess

Backing our son[2.] -Traditionally African women carry their babes on their back, using a wrapper carefully tied for the purpose. It was in Lusaka, Zambia, that friends taught me the skill and I have put it to good use. The child, carried in this way, can sleep, secure, content and close to Mum, while Mum is free to get on with tasks requiring her attention. When the child is hungry, without removing the wrapper, he/she can be gently moved to the front and access his/her mother's natural milk supply. I vividly remember "backing" my elder son Robin, when he was three and a half years old in Madrid. He was tired of walking, in the Museo del Prado where his father and I were engrossed in our admiration of Spanish art, across the centuries. Once comfortably settled on my back, all grumpy complaints ceased, Robin slept and his parents were free to continue and enjoy their visit. Yes, some Mzungu/Baturi/Oyinbo... visitors raised their eyebrows in surprise. Hopefully, they learned something and perhaps, in turn, put what they saw to good use, at a later date. This incident took place in 1973 and were I of a different skin tone, I doubt the sight would have raised eyebrows or occasioned curiosity. In 2017, in Canterbury where I live, it is not uncommon to see mothers and also fathers, walking with their infants cradled comfortable-close to their parents' bodies in factory-produced baby-carriers, a case of the West adopting and adapting time-honoured African tradtions!

This poem is based on events that occurred in the early 1940s, in the village of Aluu, some seventeen miles from Port Harcourt, in the south eastern region of Nigeria.

MADONNA AND CHILD

20th December 2016

for Irene
Canterbury City Centre, Christmas-tide 2016.

Outside, winter chill on a dreigh[1.] late afternoon,
Inside, long queues at the check-outs, restless
Customers, anxious-impatient to get home
And escape the jingle bells compulsory
Jollity, piped into ears, assaulted,
Of staff and shoppers, headache-afflicted,
Corralled in pervasive festive pressure,
Baskets and trolleys, loaded to bursting.
Behind me, a young mother, tired and harassed,
Her child strapped secure in his pushchair,
Screaming his head off, bends down to push
A rubber teat into his mouth and stem
The stares and disgruntled mutterings
Of unsympathetic, weary customers.

Then, I see at the front of the queue
A Madonna and Child, reminding me
Of African scenes and sunnier climes,
In far-away Nigeria and distant Zambia.
She stands assertive, robust and strong.
Do I detect a Yoruba accent in her voice,

When she responds to the Glasgie wifie[2.],
Processing her purchases, smiling broadly?
"This is the way we do it back home,
So I've adapted a useful habit
To the challenges of this chilly climate."

She stood regal, swathed in an all-encompassing
Thick winter coat and nestled snug inside,
With his head peeping out, a bonny boy
Of some eighteen months, smiling-content,
Warm and plump, not a care in the world.
The Glaswegian commented, as she gave
The customer her change and receipt:
"I wish someone had taught me how tae carry
My bairns[3.], comfortable-cosy, as you are doing.
All that lugging pushchairs up an' doun stairs,
When lifts were no' there, or jus' no' workin',
I could then have been spared, simply avoided.
Och, your laddie looks sae very contented
I'm wishing, I could mak' mysel' wee[4.] and join him!"
"I'd offer, if I thought there were enough room,"
Her listener, teasing-friendly responded.
So a Yoruba mother and Glaswegian granny
Discovered they shared a quick sense of humour,
Generous empathy and warm understanding,
Two women exploring their common humanity

For a few minutes, in a busy supermarket.

The Christchild would, I am sure, have approved,

Smiling down from heaven to bestow his blessing.

NOTE – dreigh[1] (varient spelling dreich), Lowland Scots, meaning wet, dull, gloomy, dismal. Standard British English has no single word to convey the combined effects of dour, drizzly weather on a dull, dreary day!

the Glasgie wifie[2] -the Glaswegian woman

My bairns[3] -my young children

mak' mysel' wee[4] -make myself small

THE LIGHT INSIDE THE DARK

1ˢᵗ May 2013

A sequence of five poems, honouring freedom voices
from the cells of Camp X-ray and in appreciation of the
work of Clive Stafford Smith and the <u>Reprieve</u> team.

NAUGHT FOR YOUR COMFORT

6ᵗʰ January 2012

Number One

for Shaker Aamer, his wife and children and for Joy
Hurcombe, Chair, of the Save Shaker Aamer Campaign

Three years ago, with a stroke of his pen,

The new super-smart hero at the helm

Signed into forthcoming oblivion

The Guantánamo Black Hole

Of "Extraordinary Rendition",

A bold start, a brave decision

To honour a pledge movingly given

And usher in a new dispensation.

Yet, three years later, we are told to accept

Those depths of despair will remain intact;

Now they will incarcerate, ad infinitum,

Suspect enemies deemed to have engaged

In hostile activities, inimical
To the almighty U.S. military.
Still, peacock-proud, the President postures
As learnèd leader of the "Free? World,"
Harvard lawyer, cool and calculating,
Of recent, electioneering-busy,
Now presidential, still eager-anxious
To promote an image of hope-and-change;
But where, tell me where, has his notion
Of restorative justice fled?
Could it have been obliterated
To extinction, by pragmatic considerations
To maintain a detention centre,
Not on U.S., but desecrated Cuban soil,
Where innocent men may be tortured,
Interrogated and interred,
Their release, a mirage, vacuous,
Indefinitely deferred?
Habeas Corpus, ejected and erased,
Is Justice, stripped naked, assaulted,
Ravaged, raped and denied,
An incendiary device, primed to explode
In war-torn countries across the world,
While in a searchlit cell of Camp X-ray,
A British resident's life drains slowly away,

After a decade of sustained misery there,

No charge to answer, because none made,

Cleared by the military overlords,

Content to exercise absolute sway

Over a man and the family

An ocean away, he knows

He may never live to see again.

To his wife, in compassion, he ceded the right

To seek a divorce, so that she and the children

Might mend broken hearts and start new lives.

The calm intensity of her reply

Shone, rainbow-radiant, in his colourless sky:

"No, I will wait for you, as long as it takes

And honour your wounded body and soul,

With the love I will keep safe for your return."

This loyalty was spoken a decade ago;

But cruelty, corrosive, continues

To take its toll, relentless and slow

On three generations of a family,

Locked into impotent frustration and woe.

Meanwhile, smug in his Oval Office, alone

The President considers the about-turn

That even his well-oiled Predecessor

Would have lacked the audacity to perform.

Could it be that the old agenda

Was never really driven out of town,

Just hidden, til the excitement died down?

An unpalatable truth will out:

All that hopeful talk of change was spin,

A war economy needs wars to win;

And lest we forget, an offshore Black Hole

Is always useful to disappear prisoners in.

As for the Geneva Conventions,

Like Habeas Corpus, they don't mean a thing

In the RepDem games of Washington D.C.!

NOTE – When President Obama was awarded the Nobel Peace Prize, after only nine months in office, Cornel West commented:
"Following Brother Martin King, we know
that peace is not the absence of conflict.
Peace is the presence of justice."

SEE – The New Statesman. 9th January, 2012, p.31.

and Paul Cahalan, "Obama's U-turn on Guantánamo seals fate of lone Briton," The Independent On Sunday, 1st January, 2012, p.3.

BREAKING THE SILENCE

8th January 2012

Number Two

A question insists
Bombarding the heart,
Beating on the brain,
Staining my cheeks
With the sting of shame,
For the President has consigned,
With insouciant disdain,
Three generations of a family
To a living hell,
Their present and future
Stolen from them,
Sentenced to suffering
In silent prisons
Of perpetual pain.
Let the President and
Prime Minister of the U.K.
Take time to visit Camp X-ray
And explain to Shaker Aamer
Why he and his family
Are tortured in this way?

Where Injustice rules, entrenched,

Democracy dies yet again,

An insult to every decent citizen,

Leaving a legacy of anger and hate

For the innocent-unborn to inherit,

So that wars-without-end

May proliferate unchecked.

NOTE – Breaking silence is a simple expression of solidarity with a prisoner, unlawfully and indefinitely separated from his family, a continent and ocean away, by the actions and inaction of U.S. and U.K. institutions, reminding me of the theme underpinning Wole Soyinka's 1972 account of imprisonment during the Biafran/Nigerian Civil War (1967-1970), namely the imperative to resist and repudiate injustice, for the man dies in all who keep silent, in the face of tyranny. Indeed, women share the same responsibility!

SEE – The Man Died. Wole Soyinka. Harmondsworth: Penguin Books Ltd., 1975.

SUGGESTION
or
CHANGE WE CAN BELIEVE IN

Number Three

for Clive Stafford Smith and the <u>Reprieve</u> team

Since Peace is the presence of Justice
Not Justice absent, ignored,
Refused or indefinitely deferred,
Wouldn't the Nobel Peace Prize Committee
Be well advised to withdraw
Their sullied Twenty Ten Award,
Recover the prize money, then see it conferred
On another lawyer and his diligent team,
Working to disinter from their prison tombs
The innocent victims of oil wars obscene?

THE LIGHT INSIDE THE DARK

27th April 2013

Number Four

The prisoner speaks with stark,
Calm authority, simple words
Against the banal depravity,
Unleashed systematic,
First, to break his helpless body,
Before attempting subjugation of
His privacy and mind,
Designed to erode, then erase
His identity, his very links
To work, home and family,
All traces of normality
Stripped away and cast aside,
Plunging him into a dark abyss,
Where past, present and future fade
Into a numbed, dulled infinity
Of more than eleven hellish years.

The prisoner's words begin
To echo elegiac round the world,
No whimpering whine of cringing defeat
But pure demand for restoration

Of freedom, stolen without reason;
And to this end, his body now yields
To self-imposed, starvation,
A potent proclamation
That he will endure, no more,
The long sustained assault
On his cornered, captured soul;
And soon, many prisoner-brothers
Choose to join his simple strike action,
Their sense of isolation diminished
As the light inside the darkness grows,
Faint glimmer brightening to shared glow,
Giving him strength to send words,
Asking for stoïcal acceptance,
Of the hard road he has chosen,
From the wife and children
Suffering so much, so long,
Even the one he has never seen,
Or held, or touched, or known.

And how to warn of the sudden storm
That might invade their hearts and home,
How to prepare their wounded minds,
That his body might not survive
The consequences of a long hunger strike,
Already reaching eighty days and nights?

Yet, when they come, the words resonate,
Clear and compelling, direct truth-telling:
If Death prevents our reunion on earth,
Remember, I did not die a coward;
In demanding Freedom-and-Justice,
I refuse the ignominy of silence,
Of prostrating and begging
For what is rightfully ours,
Unlawfully seized and stolen
By terror-intoxicated tyrants.
I can only hope, in my action,
You will find a measure of solace
And something you and our children
May at least, at last be proud of.

And if I should step off that plane
Enabling me, at last, to hold
All of you in my arms again,
I shall not cease to claim my right
To speak truth in a court of law,
So that the network of torturers
Can be seen for what they really are,
Purveyors of terror, in the service of war.
And why must it take so long to learn
That torture's harvest yields loss after loss,
Truth buried in a welter of limping lies,

Pain-induced false confessions

Breeding new generations

Of vengeful terrorists?

And surely, you and I

And our darling children,

And all the world's children

Deserve to inherit a legacy

So much better than this filthy depravity?

NOTE – During the Biafran/Nigerian Civil War (1967-1970), Wole Soyinka spent nearly two years in solitary confinement, his imprisonment a response, on the part of Federal Military Authorities to his anti-war activism. On the tenth day of his hunger strike, he wrote the following, concluding lines to the poem "I Anoint My Flesh:"

"...I anoint my heart
Within its flames I lay
Spent ashes of your hate-
Let evil die."

SEE – A Shuttle In The Crypt. Wole Soyinka. London: Rex Collings/Eyre Methuen, 1972, p.19.

LEAVETAKING

Number Five

My body refuses this gulag cell,
My mind intent on breaking the spell.
Already, my leavetaking has begun,
Propelled by the sacred hunger
To embrace the wife imprisoned
In separation, a sentence inflicted
Wordless by evil, invisible forces
On a Mother having no reply,
No resolution to her children's cry:
When will our Father return to our side?
While the youngest asks, again and again:
Why can't we visit the Father I've never seen?

Tell him, I am at last on my way,
Hunger-striking, for as long as it takes,
Urging cowards to engage with their conscience
And rubber stamp my neglected release,
The only result I will readily accept,
After long years in this infernal abyss.
But if there should be no other way,
My death, the penalty exacted

By men in high office in London
And mighty Washington D.C.,
Because my silence will never be
The treacherous price I would pay
For a counterfeit, hollow liberty,
Then tell our children they can lay claim
To the honour and pride I bequeath to them,
For, no matter the manner of my leavetaking
From the torture cells of Guantánamo Bay,
My homecoming is assured, well underway
And the name we share, unbroken and fair.

NOTE – 1.) In attempting to convey a little of the immense courage and humanity shown by many Guantánamo detainees, I was reminded of the moving, contemporary depictions of "Les Voiles de Retour," by African artists, inspired by the spiritual concept of leavetaking-and-homecoming, shared by slaves of the Not-So-New World, i.e. the firm belief that on death, their souls would, once more, and with keen anticipation, sail across the Atlantic Ocean to be reunited, at long last with family, friends and ancestors.

2.) Articles consulted: (i) "Last British resident held in Guantánamo 'may never be allowed home'." Mark Townsend. The Observer. 21st April 2013, pp.1 and 11.

(ii) "Why can't we bring our last Guantánamo prisoner home." ibid. pp.30-31.

(iii) "Guantánamo hunger strike protest grows," Kim Sengupta. The Independent. 22nd April 2013.

(iv) "I may have to die. I hope not. I want to see my family again," Shaker Aamer. ibid. p.10.

(v) "Obama's U-turn on Guantánamo seals fate of lone Briton," Paul Cahalan. The Independent On Sunday, 1st January 2012, p.28.

(vi) BBC1, 10 P.M. News, 30th April 2013.

3.) The following information refers to the plight of prisoners, detained in Camp X-ray, in April 2013:

Of the 166 remaining prisoners detained in Camp X-ray, 100 continue to maintain their protracted hunger-strike and more than 20 are now subjected to the torture of being force-fed, prompting the recent arrival of some 40 extra medical personnel. Shaker Aamer's brave words and leadership appear to have shamed President Obama into issuing statements to the effect that he will review the situation. Since the Camp opened, more than a decade ago, there have been 6 suicides and 3 convictions, out of the 779 prisoners originally detained there. For legal, as well as political reasons, President Obama is aware that poorly informed and misinformed U.S. citizens are overwhelmingly opposed to the transfer of detainees from Guantánamo Bay to the U.S. mainland, a case of out of sight, out of mind, as one U.S. commentator opined. But perhaps no longer? The recent increase in public awareness, of the extent to which human rights abuses characterize Camp X-ray, owes much to the courageous stand taken by prisoners like Shaker Aamer and the indefatigable work of Reprieve and its Director, Clive Stafford Smith.

The Man Must Not Die, the struggle for Justice must continue.

4.) The Case of Shaker Aamer: a brief summary.

During the post 9/11 assault on Afghanistan, the school in Kabul, where he had been working as an English teacher, was bombed and destroyed. In the ensuing chaos, he was kidnapped by local, criminal opportunists, who profiteered from handing him over to the U.S. military, on the pretext that he was involved with both the Taliban and al-Qaida. Thus began his odyssey of incarceration, abuse and torture, for which he alleges British, as well as U.S. officials are responsible.

Although his release from Guantánamo was approved by both Presidents George W. Bush and Barack Obama, by April 2013, he had spent more than a decade in the Black Hole of Camp X-ray with no immediate prospect of release.

By early June (2013), Shaker Aamer and his fellow prisoners' hunger strike had entered its 4th month. By this time, 103 out of the remaining 166 prisoners were refusing food and 41 of their number subjected to being force-fed twice a day, while restrained in a chair, a process disingenuously referred to as "internal feeding" by a U.S. military spokesman at Camp X-ray. For those on hunger strike, the so-called "privilege of communal living had been withdrawn," a long-winded phrasal detour to avoid the words "solitary confinement"! Colonel John Bogden, the camp commandant, indicated to BBC reporter Jonathan Beal that tensions in the camp were running high, commenting that "all they (the prisoners) want is to go home."

SOURCE – BBC1, 10 P.M. News 6/6/2013.

Memories of another June and another history of democratic activism spring to mind. Suffragette Emily Wilding Davison died on the 8th of June 1913, 4 days after her ill-fated attempt to petition the King on Derby Day. While on hunger strike, Emily had endured 49 episodes of force-feeding. In prison, militant suffragettes demanded to be accorded the status of political prisoners, as opposed to that of common criminals. It was the refusal of prison authorities, doubtless supported by the Establishment, that led to their hunger strike and the torture of force-feeding. In a letter, Emily described feelings of suffocation and sickness, when the tube was forced down her nostrils, a procedure carried out twice a day, in an atmosphere, filled with the anguished screams of fellow sufferers. Before this humiliating cruelty, came the psychological terror of hearing the approaching footfall of the 5 or 6 men deployed to hold the prisoner down.

5.) While browsing through obituaries, in honour of Chinua Achebe, I came across a quotation from Zulu Sofola's play Wedlock Of The Gods (Ibadan: Evans, 1972):

"It is a slave who sees the truth but ties

his tongue with silence."

On the 22nd of April 2013, Shaker Aamer affirmed that despite the routine physical abuse and intimidation meted out by his gaolers:

"I refuse to be their slave."

6.) When Donald J. Trump assumed the U.S. Presidency, in January 2017, his predecessor's promise to close Guantánamo, made some 8 years earlier, had not been fulfilled. Indeed, during his presidential campaign, Donald Trump, brashly announced Guantánamo would remain open for business and, if the need arose, could be enlarged to accommodate a greater number of prisoners!

7.) On the 30th of October, 2015, after 14 years incarcerated in Guantánamo, Shaker Aamer returned home to Britain. Many ordinary, decent British citizens had campaigned over the years, for this belated end to his imprisonment and suffering. Their quiet persistence shows how the People can put pressure on elected leaders, who might otherwise maintain evasive silence and remain inactive. It is the Joy Hurcombes and Clive Stafford Smiths, who keep democracy alive in Britain and the U.S.A.

I had the opportunity to read this sequence of 5 poems during the Amnesty International Meeting, on the 12th of June, 2013, in The Friends' Meeting House, 6, The Friars, Canterbury.

PETALS OF LOVE, PART 2

7th November 2015

for Alison L.

She listened with comforting calm,
Enabling me to articulate
And, in naming, subdue the storm
Threatening disruption to my soul,
Her words, unhurried, unsentimental,
Understated, strong and gentle.
She brought me gifts to feed my mind,
For she placed my tempestuous story
In the context of evolving womankind;
And encouraged me to turn my tears to rhyme.
She listened to the music of my words,
The thrust of ideas being formed,
Honest and instinctive in her response,
When clarity demanded changes
To sketches, rough-hewn with fraying edges.
She disrupted my reclusive discontent
With scones and pots of tea and cake,
A new book to read and a bouquet
Of yellow roses, splashes sunbright
To smile on me, with promises that spring
Will come to chase weary winter away.

SHE MOVES IN BEAUTY

1st February 2016

She moves in beauty, as she charts her course,
Tending a father through his winter storms,
A husband, challenged by old-age-assaults
And his mother's need for tender support.
At times, she plays a diplomatic game,
Steering a passage between competing claims,
That rise to threaten the surface-calm
Of carefully cultivated domestic rounds;
And if, on occasion, she is taken
By surprise, failing to find the woman,
Once free to lead such a different life,
A quiet smile comes to play on her lips,
As love, in abundance, flows from her being,
Nourishing both recipient and giver,
For life, without love, is not worth the living,
A fate self-imposed by the one-per-cent,
Locked in their ghettoes of discontent,
Inured to the hurt beyond their gates.
The fate of the poor-rich holds no charm,
When love and compassion are chased out of town.
In her garden, tenderness flowers,
Through winter's tempests and summer's showers,

As she moves in beauty and charts her course,
Tending a father through his winter storms,
A husband, challenged by old-age assaults
And his mother's need for tender support;
In her house and garden, love has room to grow
For she has laboured long, to keep it so.

MOTHER AND DAUGHTER

4th May 2016

for Betty and Alison L.
Horsham 1982, London 2003, Hythe 2016.

Perhaps, it was the hardening macho-style
Of resurrected, rule-Britannia pride
That moved a Mother-of-five, to take a stand,
Though a newcomer to the market town,
Where she played midwife, to her own rebirth,
After her young ones had flown the nest
And a wounding alliance, been dissolved
From a husband loved, but deaf to her voice.
Perhaps, thoughts of her own beloved four sons,
As well as Argentinian lads and their Mums
Stirred in her, the old, unanswered, angry
Question, framed in the familiar song
She had sung with her darling daughter,
Times without number, in peaceful kitchens,
Free from the blast of exploding bombs,
Etched in the memory of a young girl,
Maturing, evolving, somehow blossoming,
Amid the strife of a war-torn century;
When will we ever learn, and why are we
Propaganda-prone, to sign up with glee

To the latest war games, that with indecent speed
Turn raucous cheers into comfortless tears?
That Sussex market town, was then a place
Of tradition-abiding country folk,
So Alison's Mum wore her dignity close,
Like a warm, protective winter coat,
Standing alone, that busy-bustling afternoon,
Her words writ bold on the placard she held,
Bearing witness to the dangers ahead.

War is not the answer, war breeds revenge
And hate, infecting generations of men,
Working men, our men and theirs,
Families, like yours and mine, trapped in distress.
This time, grant reason the strength to prevail
Against those military-industrial
Battleships, submarines and fighter planes,
Presented as symbols of national pride.
Here I stand, in silence, and rest my case,
Inviting passers-by to stay and reflect,
For surely dialogue is better than death?

It began to drizzle; drizzle turned to rain;
But still she stood, no longer afraid;
And, gradually, others came to share
Her vigil for peace, in that gathering storm,

For they knew, that if those, beating war drums, won,
The outcome would still leave matters unresolved.
This image, imprinted on her daughter's
Memory, of a Mother abandoning
Habitual shyness and reticence,
Gave that daughter, the gift of courage
To join the millions, marching in London
Against a pre-planned, illegal invasion,
That would dismember a fragile nation.
So what to do, when faced with failure,
After so many peaceful demonstrations,
The daughter pondered, perplexed and troubled?
The fear of futility hanging heavy,
World weariness draining her energy,
Closing her eyes, head in hands, unbidden
An image of calm, broke through the clouds,
As once again, she saw her younger self
Standing beside the Mother she missed,
Kettle on the boil, in the family kitchen,
Two voices rising, like songbirds in flight,
Singing for Peace, in gentle defiance.

Then a distant-familiar voice seemed to say
You are never alone, I am always here,
Open your memory box, I will appear.
Yes, the struggle is hard, but the Dream

Must live on, passed from Mother to Daughter,
From generation to generation;
Never let it be forgotten,
It is less than a century
Since the vote was won.
Remember what Emmeline, Christabel,
Sylvia and Emily Davison,
Undaunted, achieved for women of this nation.
How then, could I have sat silent, in a corner,
While our first female prime minister
Deployed her voice, strident-imperious
To pursue a bellicose agenda,
Instead of giving Peace a chance,
Through diplomatic U.N. channels.
I taught you love, and now I see you
Passing it on, in the care and devotion,
Lavished on a fragile centenarian,
A man with many a flaw as we know;
And in our topsy-turvy world
There's many a lad, calculating-cold;
But your Father was never one of those.

The daughter rose to her feet, with a spring
In her step, precious words echoing in her head,
Conscious of the currents flowing unseen,
Between time past, present and still to come,

Calling out to her Dad, I'm on my way,
Just putting your hot-choc and medicine
On the tray, pausing briefly to reflect
Love, above all, is what counts in the end;
And though her parents' paths had parted,
She knew her Mother's instincts and ethics
Prized compassion, generosity, kindness,
Over ruinous revenge, spite and malice.
Yes, love was the lesson, her Mother had taught her,
A lesson priceless, timeless, universal,
Informing the lives of the world's
Limelight-averse, exemplary citizens;
And as she carried the tray upstairs,
She smiled, secure in the knowledge
Her Mother's spirit lived within her.

NOTE – 1.) "I have learnt that a man has the right to look down on another, only when he has to help the other get to his feet." Gabriel García Márquez

2.) "The struggle of people against power is the struggle of memory against forgetting." Milan Kundera

3.) One of the songs, mother-and-daughter sang was Pete Seeger's "Where have all the flowers gone?"

4.) Both women and, in particular, Betty's daughter developed a love for gardening, growing both nourishing vegetables and beautiful plants and flowers. My Mother's garden, Alison commented, was like a beautiful painting, a kaleidoscope of vibrant colours.

FOUR POEMS IN HONOUR OF
DR. CLARA IMMERWAHR

HER TRUTH SHINES STELLAR

13th October 2015

Number One

a sequence of **four** poems to commemorate and
celebrate the life and work of Dr Clara Immerwahr
(1870-1915), and for Ursula Schönthaler.

Clara's light shines, stellar beyond the grave,
For no tomb can inter the truth she upheld,
Marrying morality and science,
In one sacred, integral endeavour,
Though the man, once beloved colleague, husband,
Father to her son, former friend and lover,
Trampled and defiled, every principle
She honoured, revered and served to the end,
When his lust for status, patriotic
Power and imperial acceptance
Broke her heart, poisoned their marriage bed;
And when, in her final defiant despair
At Fritz's refusal, to terminate
His love affair with chemical warfare,

She chose death, her memory for half a century,
Was consigned to dishonour and disgrace,
Her face, her name, excised from public space,
Because she refused to stain and betray
The pledge she made in her thirty first year,
A brilliant chemist, a woman determined
To hone her skills and serve humanity,
This vow, constant, she kept, while treachery
Hydra-headed, failed to subdue
A sweet spirit, neither patriarchy,
Nor Fatherland, nor militarism
Could asphyxiate, silence or undo.

STILL SHINES THE LIGHT

13th October 2015

Number Two

So long as there are women and men, with eyes to see,
Minds alert and hearts that can feel,
Clara's lucidity will forever shine
Into the dark spaces, where scientists,
Serving warmonger friends, remain wilfully
Blind to the hurt and harm, destroying
A myriad life forms, in casual crimes
That history may belatedly mourn,
Should reason prevail and sight be restored
To primitive men with crude, muddled minds,
Master-minding poison gas and drone attacks,
In games of conquest, on unseen lives.
Clara lived and died to bring to an end
This desecration of science
In slavish service to the god of war,
Where political imperatives,
Ill-conceived, are disguised or hidden,
Their consequences unconsidered, then ignored.

MISTRESS OF HER FATE, CAPTAIN OF HER SOUL

13th October 2015

Number Three

Fritz's dedication to the creation,

Supervision and administration

Of his toxic weapon of mass destruction

Transformed a belovèd, devoted wife

Into an enemy, imprisoned in strife,

Until with his pistol, she took her own life,

One casualty among uncounted thousands,

A new lethal harvest from the fruits of science.

Clara died in the arms of their son, Hermann,

A future victim of the legacy

His ill-fated father had begun.

A pity, my friend, dismayed, intervened,

She should have turned that gun,

On her husband instead.

But the Kaiser's men would have dispatched her,

Blindfolded, to face their firing squad;

Think of that final degradation,

Gifting the Kaiser's uniformed men

Her death, in act of public humiliation,

Came my response, to my friend's suggestion;
And though Clara died a century ago,
Her sustained condemnation of poison gas
Holds to account, a new breed of criminal
Presidents, princes, military dictators,
War profiteers and deranged terrorists,
Casual creators of uncounted corpses,
The toxic harvest of desecrated science.

FATAL IMBALANCE

14th October 2015

Number Four

I grow tired of men with a penchant for war,
Unleashing horror on both friend and foe.
Wouldn't those who nurture and care for the living
Do a far better job of ensuring
The very survival of life on earth,
For the words of peace-loving citizens
Must be acted upon, as well as heard?

Dream on Hilary, the business man said
You've got too much Utopia in your head,
Get real, turn your mind to profit instead.
But, I replied, without my dream
Of change, fundamental for the better,
I might as well be dead and buried;
And Clara's courage will have been in vain,
For her life was a symphony superb
And the parts, in harmony, sang for change,
A legacy, still sullied by bully-boys
Of little brain, from whom that legacy
Demands to be rescued, honoured, reclaimed.

The business man rode off, chauffeur driven

In a tinted-window-four-by-four,

Intimidating-aggressive, as it

Sped warrior-style on its way,

While I took to the hills, in search of fresh air,

The image of Clara, smiling at me,

Her courage, constant, through turbulent times,

Her work, in tune with common sense ideals,

Inspiring me to keep faith with my dreams.

NOTE – Clara Immerwahr (1870-1915) has been described as "a rôle model for civic courage," whose tragically short life and legacy, only began to receive appropriate public attention in Germany, some 4 decades ago.

Her surname "Immerwahr," meaning "always true" describes her life story and underlines her commitment, to the values and principles she held dear. The youngest of four children, she was born into a wealthy, liberal, German, Jewish family, becoming "the first woman to be awarded a doctorate in chemistry at a German university." On the occasion of the award ceremony, at the University of Breslau (1900), she took an oath "never in speech or writing to teach anything that is contrary to my beliefs," and "to pursue truth and to advance the dignity of science to the heights which it deserves."

The following year she married fellow chemist, Fritz Haber (1868-1934) and translated some of her husband's writing and publications into English, for which she received neither recognition nor acknowledgement. Their son Hermann was born in 1902. Further academic collaboration with Fritz, on the thermodynamics of gas reaction, led to the publication of a textbook in 1905, which he dedicated to his "beloved wife, Mrs Clara Haber, Ph. D., with thanks for quiet collaboration." The word "quiet" is indicative of the gender bias and sexist stereotyping typifying the male dominated society, with which Clara came into eloquent conflict, as a pioneering women's rights activist.

For his part, Fritz's own ambitions and social position were not immune from the undermining effects of antisemitism. "The outbreak of World War I in 1914, gave Haber an opportunity to prove his patriotism," through his energetic and "enthusiastic" focus on the development of chemical warfare and the deployment of toxic chlorine gas, as a weapon of mass destruction. Horrified and outraged, Clara expressed her opposition to this "perversion of the ideals of science." For his part, Fritz accused "her in public of making statements treasonous to the Fatherland."

"The first poison attack took place on April 22, 1915, on the Western Front in the Ypres sector of Belgium. Of the seven thousand casualties that day, more than five thousand died. Countless additional attacks resulted in the deaths of at least a hundred thousand soldiers on both sides." Fritz now basked in a sense of personal triumphalism, having been promoted to the rank of captain, in a period when Jews were denied commissions in the Prussian-dominated German army. The night, before his departure to supervise a gas attack on the Eastern Front, a bitter quarrel erupted between wife and husband. "In the early hours of May 2, 1915 Clara took her husband's pistol" and shot herself in the garden. Hermann alerted his father, who left as planned, for the Eastern Front that same day. Clara died in her son's arms. Clara's image and legacy were dishonoured, ignored and consigned to decades of oblivion for what, at the time, was regarded as a treacherous lack of patriotism on her part.

In 1918, when Fritz was awarded the Nobel Prize in chemistry, for his ground-breaking work on ammonia synthesis, the physicist Ernest Rutherford refused to shake his hand.

All above quotations from: Clara Immerwahr 1870-1915. Jewish Women's Archive. Jutta Dick. SEE reference 1.) below.

I am grateful to Ursula Schönthaler, who took time to send me information and references about Clara, after our lively conversations, in my home, had aroused my curiosity and interest, in this amazing woman. Ursula encouraged me to include Clara's story in my poems honouring "courageous women," (her phrase).

SEE – 1.) <u>Lexikon Jüdische Frauen</u>. Editors Jutta Dick and Marina Sassenberg.

<http://jwa.org/encyclopedia/article/immerwahr-clara>.

2.) <u>Der Fall Clara Immerwahr</u>. Ein Leben für eine humane Wissenschaft. Gerit von Leitner. München: 1993.

3.) <u>Die Hälfte des Lebens, femina doctissima Clara Immerwahr</u> (television documentary)

4.) <u>Clara Immerwahr</u> – Wikipedia, the free encyclopedia

<http://en.wikipedia.org/wiki/Clara_Immerwahr>.

5.) <u>Square Rounds</u>. Tony Harrison. London: Faber and Faber, 1992. (A play in verse, song and dance, which asks: How did the utopian promise of science lead to the release of chemical weapons?) The play was first performed at the Olivier Theatre, London, in October 1992.

ASPIRATION

13th April 2016

"I want people in Syria to carry a pen, not a sword,"
words of a Syrian refugee.

We live with the scars of past encounters,
Walking wounded, on a wounded planet,
Caught in the horns of an old dilemma:
To follow our dreams, or choose compromise,
Burying cherished ideals in forests of lies,
Where the excited anticipation
Of privileged, conspicuous consumption,
Divides and disrupts the disgraced human race,
Making monsters of children bred to command,
Demand and inherit, what was never theirs,
While millions face war, hunger, disease,
Their tears trickling silent, down hollow cheeks;
Yet, should we dare to speak truth to power
And reclaim government for the People,
Refusing to submit, to propaganda
Promoting imperial misadventure,
Corporate greed and devastation,
We could break free from the tyranny
Of successive forms of slavery,
Addiction to war, aversion to peace,

And usher in a bold new beginning,

Common wealth and co-operation

Guiding, empowering the Common People

To ensure, happiness in abundance,

Smiles on the faces of the world's children,

Taught to care for each other and heal the hurt

Too long inflicted on the planet of their birth;

And this, surely, of necessity must be

The definition of democracy,

Children smiling, secure and at ease,

Learning to care for the world at their feet.

NOTE – This poem is for Dr Sinan al-Rawi and the Syrian refugee girl, whose humanity endures beyond the horror of losing home and members of her family. When asked to articulate her hope for the future, she replied: "I want the world's children to be happy."

Thank you, Sinan, for bringing her indomitable humanity to my attention. She became the inspiration for this poem. Because of unsung heroines like her, we have to do better. Her life embodies the urgent message in W. H. Auden's iconic lines on the outbreak of World War Two. The poet's voice, he asserts, is all that he/she has "to undo the folded lie," to become "a point of light," "an affirming flame" in "darkened lands;" but this Syrian refugee girl IS "an affirming flame." Her truth exposes "the folded lie," IS "a point of light," in "the darkened lands" of the earth; and amid the offending "odour of death," she retains the capacity to love.

Those eight words, "I want the world's children to be happy," should be tattooed on the foreheads of the world's military madmen, arms traders, zealots and political misleaders.

SEE – Another Time. W. H. Auden. London: Faber and Faber, 2007 edition. pp.103-106.

INTEGRITY

16th March 2017

for Ken Loach, Paul Laverty and team.

He came out of retirement
And made "I, Daniel Blake,"
Not because he was chasing
Celebrity-recognition in Cannes,
(That prize, a happy, unexpected surprise)
But because outrage at the state
Of our divided nation
And the plight of the Poor,
Vilified and despised
By the robber-rogues,
Ruling rapacious-indecent
Over us all, stirred his spirit,
Ignited his creativity,
Forced him at eighty
To call on his comrades, pick up his camera,
And hold up a mirror to society,
Reflecting the calculated cruelty,
At the heartless centre
Of a labyrinthine bureaucracy,
Designed to discourage victim-applicants
From seeking the help they are entitled to,

Using his skills to empower
Voices, suppressed or ignored,
To speak truths, painful, essential,
Uncensored, reaching across borders
Erected to distract and confuse the People
And lock their assaulted sensibilities,
Inside constructs of prejudiced ignorance,
Travelling the length and breadth
Of our Disunited Queendom,
Listening, recording, validating,
Comparing searing, untold stories,
Employing those who live them
To perform them for all of us,
Creativity at work, produced with love,
Urgent anger, empathy, compassion,
Creativity of the People,
By the People, for the People
Of a confused, troubled,
Post-imperial, class-divided,
Northern European nation,
Still failing to transition into
A Commonwealth, peaceful-sustainable
Of civilized, co-operative citizens,
For a nation that functions to serve
A greedy local-global-one-per-cent

Is designed to produce misery,

Alienation, discontent

Among the growing numbers of dispossessed.

Now is the Hour and now the Time

To defend the rights, usurped,

Of Daniel Blake and the millions

Disenfranchised by that corrupt-cold-élite.

CODA: Such A Parcel Of Rogues In Westminster

Our former Austerity-Finance-Minister

Now a back bencher on a modest

Seventy-Four-Thousand pound salary,

Has of recent been busy amassing

An additional One-And-A-Half Million,

Through his lucrative business connections,

Well, after all, he is a talented

Man of prodigious skill and energy,

Able to do so much more with his time,

Than merely attend to his constituency,

While on the other side of his Great-Divide

The Daniel and Daniella Blakes multiply

Legally deprived of meagre benefits,

Increasingly difficult to access.

NOTE – 1.) I am, once again, reminded of what the founder of a
U.S. automobile company once said: "It is well enough that people
of the nation do not understand our banking and monetary system,

for if they did, I believe there would be a revolution before tomorrow morning." Henry Ford (1863-1947)

2.) In one of his "Letter(s) From America" re-broadcast on the BBC World Service on the 29th July, 2002, Alistair Cooke quoted the steel magnate Andrew Carnegie, on the issue of wealth accumulation and distribution: "The problem of our age is the proper administration of wealth." Andrew Carnegie (1835-1919)

3.) Emeritus Professor Noam Chomsky has argued that democratic change at international level cannot occur without "informed global public opinion," playing a dynamic rôle in redressing the balance of power between the U.S.A. and other nation states. The same prerequisite applies at local, regional and national levels.

SEE – Hegemony Or Survival. Noam Chomsky. London: Hamish Hamilton, 2003, p.59.

May I suggest that Ken Loach's work from "Cathy Come Home," to "I, Daniel Blake" is designed to inform public opinion, on many levels local, regional, national and international. In our time, the public is too often ill-served, mis-and-disinformed by the sections of the media and press, in the pocket and on the payroll of the infamous local-global-one-per-cent.

4.) When Ken Loach was recently accused by a Conservative M.P., on BBC's Newsnight, of gross exaggeration in his film "I, Daniel Blake," with steely calm, he replied that his team had come across even more extreme cases of injustice, than those depicted in his film and cited the experience of a young woman who, having suffered a heart attack during a gruelling interview, conducted by a Social Security official and who, unlike the tragic hero of Ken Loach's film, had survived her attack, was, none the less, denied "benefits" on the grounds that she had failed to complete her interview! By way of response, both the television interviewer and Tory M.P. were bereft of words.

This charge of exaggeration featured prominently in the right-wing media, indeed, by many who offered condemnatory comments without even having seen the film!

OF SILENCE AND BIAS

On Saturday the fourth of March,
A quarter of a million marched
On London's streets, in defence
Of a public health service,
In mortal danger, under siege;
But on public service television
And radio stations, funded by the People,
The event received barely a mention,
Swiftly sidelined, buried in silence,
While angry voices across the Land
Call for this wanton destruction to end,
Demanding our N.H.S. be rescued
From profiteering privatization,
A process, cumulative, enacted
Against the wishes of the People
Unconsulted, in typical fashion,
First by complicit New Labour bosses,
Followed by imperious Bullingdon Boys[1.]
Riding roughshod over the rest of us,
Telling us their policies are simply
Austerity-inevitable,
Rather than a calculated procedure,

For stealthily planned decline,
Mapping a route to the ultimate demise
Of a public service underfunded,
Held to ransom, up-for-grabs.

For too long, the People, compliant,
Have been coaxed and lulled into passivity,
By garish distractions, bombarding the senses,
Dulling the mind into confused apathy,
Yet, if the extent of privatization
Over decades of theft by stealth
And relentless erosion was understood,
No Prime Minister would slumber
Peaceful in Number Ten,
Until the People's representatives
Were made to undo the harm they are doing,
The harm they have done, while masquerading
As loyal, principled public servants,
Hiding their rôle as conniving asset strippers,
Aiming to please both themselves
And their hedge-fund friends in the City[2].
On the first Saturday of March 2017,
A quarter of a million marched on London streets;
But how many more millions must raise
Their voices, determined, adamant
That these acts of élite vandalism

Must cease, forthwith, the perpetrators

Brought to book, divested of their stolen loot,

Restored to the People, from whom it was taken,

Restored to them, for the Common Good?

<u>NOTE</u> – the Bullingdon Boys[1.] -an élitist Oxford University club, to which, inter alia, our present Foreign Secretary, former Prime Minister and former Chancellor of the Exchequer belonged, in their student days. Several years ago, I saw a clip from a documentary film, showing a group of Bullingdon Boys, emerging from an expensive restaurant, in a somewhat inebriated state, nothing remarkable in that, you will say, except that British television programmes constantly regale us with images of the inebriated, much maligned "undeserving poor," and rarely images of super-privileged members of the Establishment, sozzled (slang, meaning drunk) and misbehaving. In the clip, we see one undergraduate, detach himself from his group of friends, to stop and taunt a less fortunate fellow-citizen, begging for money, on a cold winter's night. The Bullingdon Boy, in question, ostentatiously withdraws a £5 or £10 note from his wallet, tears it in half and proceeds to set it on fire with his cigarette lighter, directly in front of the supplicant, a man at least twice or thrice his age. The image has haunted me. As a nasty manifestation of ageism and class division, it led me back in time to the worlds of Hans Christian Andersen's much loved story "<u>The Little Match Girl</u>" and that depicted by his friend Charles Dickens' in "<u>Oliver Twist</u>." Social change can simultaneously move in different directions: think of the amazing speed of technological innovation, think of the equally dramatic increase in social and economic inequality!

That clip also reminded me of a lesson taught to me, by a dear friend some years ago, when she was in her late seventies. We were walking through Canterbury's West Gate, after an early evening meal, in the Café des Amis du Mexique, when she drew my attention to a beggar, slumped in front of the entrance to the West Gate museum. I told Elizabeth, that in such situations, I preferred to give food rather than money, to avoid the possibility of the donation being spent on alcohol or drugs. Elizabeth, a lady of strong principles, who had brought up seven children as a single parent, survived domestic abuse and, in extremis, sought sanctuary in our local Women's Refuge, worked as a nurse until reaching the age of retirement, sang lustily in her church and two other choirs... cast a disapproving, nay withering look in my direction and pointed out, that if one of us were homeless, unemployed and dealing with some terrible trauma or tragedy, we too might seek temporary escapism, and she concluded, as a follower of Christ, she was not about to judge the most vulnerable in society. I duly unzipped my purse and told my friend she was a better teacher than I was. It is life that is the greatest of teachers, yes, life and what we make of our experiences, she concluded.

the City[2] -the name given to the part of London, where many important financial institutions have their main offices.

Just over a decade ago, the Portuguese Nobel-Laureate José Saramago commenting on the anti-war demonstrations in London, before and after the illegal, immoral U.S. led invasion of Iraq in 2003, made the following pertinent points (He was living in Madrid at the time):

"In Madrid and London, we marched, we did our duty, then we went home and those in power" took no notice. "But we have to keep on demonstrating, and demonstrating and demonstrating – there's no solution but to say we do not want to live in a world like this with wars, inequality, injustice, the daily humiliation of millions of people, who have no hope that life is worth anything. We have to express it with vehemence and spend days on the street if we have to, until those in power recognise that the people are not happy,"

and, let me add, so that measures are taken to change the political, social and economic conditions responsible for that unhappiness. Why, we must ask, are certain governments reluctant to spend the People's money on public services, such as health, and fund them to a high standard, while finding money for illegal, military interventions and misadventures, with indecent ease and speed?

José Saramago, in his first interview with a British newspaper, concluded:

"We're not short of movements proclaiming that a different world is possible; but unless we can co-ordinate them into an organic international movement, capitalism just laughs at all these little organisations" that, on their own, have little impact. "The problem is that the right doesn't need any ideas to govern, but the left can't govern without ideas. It's very difficult."

SEE – <u>The Observer Review</u>. 30th April 2006, p.24.

AGEISM or DIGNITY DENIED

28th May 2011

In Britain, the elderly are expected

To apologize for being old,

Defer to the young and do what they're told.

Instead of being dustbinned

In profiteering "care homes,"

Should they not have the right

To decide when to exit, with dignity,

From the crass tyranny of an ageist world?

NOTE – A Tanzanian proverb reminds us:
    What you are, we once were,
    What we are, you will become.

WEALTH MISAPPROPRIATED,
IN A STATE MALADMINISTERED

25th March 2017

Integrity, a rare commodity
In corridors of self-serving power,
Is visibly absent, on the luxury
Yachts of billionaire entrepreneurs,
Their wealth, purloined from workers
Who have ceased to serve their purpose,
Abruptly abandoned to insecurity,
Unemployment, broken promises and contracts,
While those who stole their futures from them
Cruise in opulence, their loot locked up
In secretive-safe, hospitable tax havens,
Where wives' accounts come in nice-and-handy.
In the Disunited Queendom,
Such glittering careers are honoured
With ceremonies in Buckingham Palace
And acquisition of distinguished titles.
What honest man or woman would wish,
In such unsavoury circumstances,
To receive a British dame-or-knighthood?

I'd rather such honours were awarded
To overworked, underpaid homecare providers,

Helping the elderly retain a measure
Of independence and personal dignity.
Now don't forget, a friend reminded me,
Those homecare providers are, all too often,
Victims of private, profiteering companies,
Making fortunes, for the rogues who own them!
In which case I, ruefully, replied:
Both careworker and cared-for
Are victims, imprisoned in the same
System of pervasive exploitation,
Politely referred to, as the Private Sector,
While Public has become the despised,
Disinherited, poor relative.
Isn't the time long overdue
To redress the balance,
Before the Ship of State
Capsizes, or carries the nation
Onto the rocks of disintegration,
After a debilitating hangover
And lingering, mistaken nostalgia,
For the demise of a core-rotten empire,
That treated its home-grown, industrial workers,
Its colonial subjects and resources,
As material, ripe for profit-extraction,
Concentrated privilege and smug ostentation

Expanding, alongside the proliferation
Of slum poverty and squalor,
Workers, pittance-paid, disempowered,
Deprived of their rightful share
In the wealth, they had created,
On which that ostentation smugly rested?

The past is alive in the present,
Will persist, pernicious, into the future,
Unless and until, history is understood
From the Peoples' perspectives and experiences,
Not unofficially censored and distorted,
To secure the continuing interests
Of over-privileged, vainglorious victors,
Stealing the limelight from those
Who labour to keep the lights on.
History must be rescued from the clutches
Of marauding minority interests,
The men and women, playing dishonest games
With the Common People, they cheat and deceive,
Within a Dickensian-style legal system,
Increasingly inaccessible
To those, on no-or-low wage incomes.
The world is tired, impatient
For this nightmare, persistent, to end,
A nightmare, wounding, impoverishing

The beautiful planet, plundered at will,

By techno-crude predators, out of control,

Deaf, dumb and blind, to the harm that they do.

NOTE – Over recent weeks, we have been made aware of a crisis affecting homecare providers, working from 7 A.M. in the morning til 9 P.M. at night, on low pay (£7.55 per hour), often on zero hours contracts, receiving no, or inadequate, fuel allowance, denied adequate travel time between clients, so that a client having paid for half an hour of care, may receive a meagre fifteen minutes, leaving both client and carer frustrated, angry and resentful. In addition, the carer is required to write and often telephone notes to her employer, before completing each visit. Consequently, by 2016, thousands of homecare providers had handed in their notice and left their jobs, many expressing anger that intolerable working conditions had made it impossible for them to deliver the quality of service that vulnerable, elderly clients had paid for and had a right to expect. In short, a combination of stress, exhaustion, poor remuneration and job dissatisfaction has escalated to crisis point, in a context where unhappy care worker and unhappy senior citizen function, as "human resources" for profiteering minorities. They are people, individuals not "human resources"!

A MARRIAGE OF TRUE MINDS

14th April 2017

for Elke and Karl
Baden-Würtemberg, Southern Germany

In her village, the way of thinking
Seemed purpose-designed to stifle
Her potential, consign her, unwilling,
To early marriage and round-after-round
Of dull, all-consuming domestic duties.
Over years, it was made dogmatic-clear,
That her brothers would, by right, inherit
The family vineyards, wine-making business,
Trained and educated, express for this purpose.
At the age of nineteen, she packed her bags,
Determined to resolve the impasse,
Speaking assertive to her parents
Of plans made, action about to be taken.
No hysterical, melodramatic scenes
Were allowed to disrupt her calmly
Stated rational decision,
To continue her formal education,
Follow her dreams and discover
Where they might lead, where they might take her.

In a student hall of residence, she met
A young man determined, thoughtful and strong,
With a story, curious-troubling,
Surprisingly, not unlike her own,
His situation, reflecting the very reverse
Of the impasse that had blocked her path,
But, at the root, the same frustration,
Parents locked within rigid expectations,
His family, determined he pursue
A successful, keen-competitive
Business career, where his leadership
Potential, energy driven and directed,
Would shine for all the world to see and admire,
His steady ascent up the ladder
Of wealth and enhanced social status,
Badges of success that would make them feel proud.

When she inhaled a delicious aroma
Escaping, tantalizing, from his room,
She knocked on the door he had left ajar,
And, somehow, the conversation had led
To a lively meal, she would never forget,
Impressed by his creative, culinary skills,
His unexpected, generous offer
To share his love of inspired cooking,
With an inquisitive, hungry stranger.

Sometime later, he told her the tale
Of how his bicycle had been damaged
On its journey by train, how the station
Master dismissed his request for redress,
Disclaiming company responsibility,
His rebuff, an arrogant assumption
That the young man standing in front of him
Was himself the author of the damage,
Trying his luck, just a lad on the make.
Magdalene's anger led to action;
She noted the details with factual
Precision and swiftly drafted a claim
For compensation, for him to make use of
At his discretion. Now he was the one
Grateful-surprised by her care, her kindness,
Impressed by her efficient defence
Of his consumer rights, her sense that
Fair play and justice should by law
Be accessible to every German citizen.
Well, she quipped, I've done nothing special,
Just thought, that if your bike were mended,
We might enjoy some rides together!
So it was, they made a pact; he did the cooking,
She took care of bureaucratic paper work.
Cooking, she confessed, I try to avoid,

Have never enjoyed, though told I should!
Form filling and bureaucratic procedures
Bore me to tears, give me a headache, he replied.
My weakness, my long-held aversions
Are your strength, whet your appetite
For speedy action and efficient resolution.
Don't you think, he laughed and smiled,
We're simply tailor-made for each other;
And now that my bike is in good shape,
Think of all those rides we can take!
Yes, they agreed, her rumbling stomach,
His paper work procrastination
Had brought into being, a lovely
Unexpected, symbiotic friendship,
Each exploring what they found
To appreciate and treasure in the other,
Free from the judgemental stereotyping
And pressure, each had experienced at home,
Refusing to submit, refusing to conform.

Their joy in self-and-mutual discovery
Found expression in music and dancing,
Not only from Bach to The Beatles,
Gershwin to Dylan, but also Brazilian Salsa,
Congolese Rhythms and Cuban Rumba.
So it was, that six weeks to the day they first met,

This young man and woman decided to wed;
And though she was a lass of twenty,
He a lad of twenty one, their partnership
Was founded on gender equality
And a sensible, firm agreement
That if, in future, they were blessed with children,
Whoever earned the higher salary
Would assume the rôle of financial provider,
The other becoming principal homemaker.

Seven years later, when their first son was born,
Magdalene had become the business partner
Of a Greek medical entrepreneur,
Who had used his skills and expertise
To develop a range of cosmetics
Using authentic, natural ingredients,
While Magdalene took care of promotion,
Marketing and distribution.
Before her maternity leave came to an end,
Her husband allayed her doubts and fears:
Since you earn more than I, and derive
Satisfaction from the business you run,
There can be no doubt, it is crystal clear,
You must be the principal breadwinner,
I, the fully engaged, home-based breadmaker.
You work for a company you co-founded,

Nurturing its growth and development,
For this you must travel, holding seminars,
Exploring new markets far from home,
Crossing borders into Ukraine and Russia.

Their two sons, now university graduates,
Were taught domestic skills and self-reliance
By their Father. Why, yes, he smiles, mischievous,
One day they might cook, nearly as well as I do;
But more than this, together, my Wife and I
Have taught them empathy, co-operation,
How to live life to the full,
Think independently, love nature,
Care for the world, we take too much for granted,
Honour their girlfriends, for their unique potential,
Just as we appreciate Magdalene
For her courage, industry, tenacity.
As for me, I have built a nest, strong, protective,
A place of shelter and nourishing laughter.
Then, Magdalene adds, with love in her eyes,
Without my husband's strength, and devotion
To our boys, I would never have achieved
My position as company director, now owner;
And what we have made of our opportunities
Proves that gender rôles can be varied and flexible,
For my love's choice of lifestyle, made mine possible.

He is my partner, my soul-mate, my belovèd;
And though we married when we were young,
Our marriage has stood the test of time;
And the same cannot be said of some,
Quick to criticize us, with spiteful tongues;
And still of an evening, when I am home,
We choose music we love and dance til dawn,
Celebrating that meeting four decades ago,
When a young man and woman
Found freedom and fulfilment,
Through the love that brought
And keeps them together.

EMPIRE IN CRISIS

15th November 2016

My pain is a sacred flame,
A link in an ancient chain,
Broken, then reforged
In a cycle repetitive,
Between freedom unfettered
And slavery reinstated,
As cruelty smiles,
Brazen-unconcerned,
From corporate towers
Thrusting, contemptuous,
Into raped, garish skies,
Stolen wealth and usurped power
Playing twisted games theatrical,
With brittle-broken men and women,
The discarded detritus
Of an empire in crisis,
State-gangster-capitalism
Holding the line, against
The anger of the Common People,
In the struggle between
Justice and tyranny.
Yet, in these times of blighted lives,

Democracy invoked, democracy denied,

Let us remember Shelley's line[1.]:

We are many, they are few;

And on the many, depend the few.

For this reason, propaganda rages

To confuse the many and create false enemies.

NOTE – Shelley's line[1.] -I have adapted the original line, replacing "Ye" with "We," but the meaning and sentiment remain the same.

SEE – The Mask of Anarchy Written on the Occasion of the Massacre at Manchester, Percy Bysshe Shelley (1792-1822), the words I refer to form the concluding line of his poem, which has been called Shelley's "rallying hymn to non-violent resistance" and is an impassioned response to the Peterloo Massacre of 1819, when militiamen charged protestors, who had assembled in St Peter's Field, Manchester, campaigning for increased voting rights, in an era when voting was the exclusive privilege of wealthy male landowners. There were at least six fatalities and it is estimated some five hundred demonstrators were injured, including women and children.

Here then are the poem's concluding lines, addressed directly to the Common People:

"Rise like Lions after slumber
In unvanquishable number -
Shake your chains to earth like dew
Which in sleep had fallen on you -
Ye are many – they are few."

A Choice of Poets (New Edition). Editor Dr David Edwards. Walton-on-Thames: Thomas Nelson & Sons Ltd., 1999, pp.86-88.

WHAT THIS WORLD NEEDS NOW

3rd October 2016

for Sir David Attenborough, Burt Bacharach and
Professor Stephen Hawking.

As I write, the world lies wounded, bleeding
How many species and unknown life forms
Have we, careless, hurled over the precipice,
Driven, undiscovered, unrecorded,
Into premature extinction,
Blind to our stupendous stupidity,
Our incapacity to love and care for
The shining, irreplaceable planet we live on?
Are we never to evolve beyond
Such primitive modes of high-tech-unthinking?
Do we have to wait, active-passive,
For self-replicating forms
Of independent artificial intelligence,
Cold-robotic, logic-driven, super-fast
Powerful calculating thought systems,
To consign US, helpless, premature,
Into our own self-generated extinction?
We are creatures, global-interconnected,
Yet never more lonely, more isolated,
Quick-clever beings, bereft of wisdom,

Dazzled, dazed by the accelerating
Speed of techno-change and innovation,
Hubris-drunk, on our seeming-infinite
Expanding powers of endless invention.
Turn we must and look, unflinching,
At the legacy, lunatic,
Of unimpeded human folly.
I would replace this nightmare, monstrous,
With my dream for a saner, kinder tomorrow.
What the world, in sheer desperation, needs
Is what has always been in shortest supply,
Healing love and unimpeded caritas
For our scarred, irreplaceable jewel in the sky.

REMEDIAL ACTION

18th March 2017

(should be taken to a certain, well padded presidential
bahoochie[1.])

If Donald's Mum had been around
To witness her son's surly arrogance,
Refusing, before the world's press and cameras
To shake the hand of his guest in the White House,
Her strang, Scottish working class response
Would have been to soundly spank his bahoochie
And send him to bed without any supper,
Then in the morning, before tea and porridge,
He would have been made to compose
A lengthy, WELL WRITTEN letter of apology.
Let journalists and social media magnates
Turn their backs and block publicity access
To such coarse, juvenile, bully-boy antics;
And we know, had his guest been of a younger,
Luscious, curvaceous-glamorous appearance,
He would have done more than hold her hand,
Had opportunity been his to command.
How can such a man, with scant regard
For womankind and the office he holds,
Be allowed to pursue an agenda,

Macho-militaristic, flippantly

Adding to the suffering and woes

Of babes and children,

Starving or blitzkrieged[2.]

In far-flung Yemen, Iraq,

Afghanistan and Syria?

Where are the citizens, with courage and principle,

Who will peacefully apply remedial action

And provide an antidote, to this poisonous

Delusion-driven, false nationalism?

NOTE – bahoochie[1.] –[bəxuːxɪ], bottom, buttocks, arse, Lowland Scots, informal usage.

blitzkrieged[2.] -a blitzkrieg is a fast, intense military attack, designed to surprise the enemy and secure rapid victory. The compound German noun "blitzkrieg" comprises the words, "blitz," meaning lightning with "krieg," meaning war. I wanted to use the compound word as an adjective, so employing poetic licence, I added the -ed ending!

This poem was prompted, in part, by President Trump's refusal to shake the German Chancellor's hand, in the full glare of the world's media, on the occasion of her official visit to Washington, on the 17th of March. She was heard, whispering to her host in a low diplomatic tone, "What about the handshake?" her host played deaf, and ignored his guest's astonished reminder. If manners maketh the man, the billionaire business man, turned politician, is unmade, unmannerly, ill-suited to the Office he holds, in which any manifestation of misogynist prejudice should be given short shrift. I wonder how many hands Queen Elizabeth must have shaken, over the decades, belonging to men, whose company she might well have preferred to avoid!

Anthony Baxter has made two powerful documentaries on the Trump phenomenon, world and values he represents. The first film, entitled "You've been trumped," Montrose Pictures Ltd. 2012, received 10 major awards. Michael Hogan, described the documentary as "stunning and emotionally potent," in The Daily Telegraph; Mark Kermode, BBC film critic, called it "brilliant;" Michael Moore commented "It blew me away," while the man himself responded with the words "A failure!"

SEE – www.youvebeentrumped.com

STILL IN CONTENTION

22nd April 2017

for Gustave

Once, a Roman temple claimed that space,
In honour of Janus-and-Jana,
The twin-headed Guardian-Deity of Gates,
Linked with New Year and new beginnings
And the interchanging possibilities
Of Rome's turbulent victories and miseries,
Fluctuating, imperial, between
Alternating periods of War and Peace,
The tidal momenta of arrogant
Expansion, sullen-yielding to decline
And slow, inexorable contraction.
Next, came a Christian temple, modest
In size, of Visigoth origin.
Then, came conquering Arabs and Berbers,
So the temple was strictly divided,
Two spaces, designated exclusive
For either Christian or Moslem,
Though one could argue, both were united
Under one sky, one roof comprehensive,
Covering that enforced separation;
But, Emir Abd al Rahman the First

Determined to combine secular
And religious pre-eminence,
In a statement, visual-impressive,
Of imperial reach and permanence.
First, he purchased the Christian half,
Before bringing the entire edifice
Tumbling down, and in its place overseeing
The construction of the Grand Mosque of Córdoba.
Four and a half centuries later,
Came the Spanish Reconquista,
One empire expiring, another rising,
Religion, an expression of imperial rivalry.
In time, a nave was introduced
Within the framework of the Mosque,
And the minaret, adapted to function
As the bell tower, summoning
The Roman Catholic faithful to enter
And worship in pious, cathedral splendour.
Today in twenty seventeen, officials
Can, on occasion, be seen enforcing
A rigid status quo, ordering Moslem
Visitors, kneeling to offer their prayers,
That they must desist, or exit and leave.
I would rather Spanish politicians
And lawmakers, look again at the effects

Of exclusion, engendering
Mistrust, fear, ignorance and worse,
For the flames of zealotry and hatred
Are all too easily ignited and fanned
By scenes of public humiliation,
Rejection, authorized by religion.
Who would choose to sit in a garden
Filled with flowers of one sole colour?
Who can imprison his mind, in a cell
Of sacerdotal dogma and sterility
And robed in blinkered, smug hypocrisy
Claim to serve the interests of humanity?
The barriers and barricades, erected
By fearful, tyrannical thought-police
Should be dismantled, with utmost speed,
So that we can share and appreciate
What by right, belongs to all of us,
And take better care of Mother Earth.

NOTE – 1.) Over the last two decades, Spanish Moslems have been lobbying the Roman Catholic Church to give them permission to pray in the place of worship, universally referred to as Córdoba's Mezquita-Catedral/Mosquée-Cathédrale/Mosque-Cathedral... To date, these efforts have proved unsuccessful. The history of Cordoba's Mezquita-Catedral, 711 to date (2017), is complex, contradictory and, hopefully, still evolving.

2.) "At Rome, Numa (the legendary second king of that city) is said to have dedicated to Janus the covered passage bearing his name,

which was opened in times of war and closed in times of peace....
It appears to have been left open in war, to indicate symbolically
that the god had gone out to assist the Roman warriors, and to have
been shut in times of peace that the god, the safeguard of the city,
might not escape." New Year's day was the principal festival of the
god, when presents were exchanged "consisting of sweetmeats and
copper coins."

SEE – <u>A Smaller Classical Dictionary Of Biography, Mythology
and Geography</u>. William Smith, D.C.L. and LL. D., London: John
Murray, 1874 (15th Edition), pp.225. and 287.

3.) Just as Roman imperialist rhetoric and propaganda invoked
symbolic support from the god Janus, we heard former U.S. President George W. Bush employ the word "crusade," in the toxic
propaganda prefacing the illegal invasion of Iraq, in March 2003.

In 1963, Bob Dylan's anti-war exposé of U.S. militarism
stormed the senses, as the verses of his song "<u>With God On Our
Side</u>" offered a narrative, charting the history of a U.S. imperium
consistently and persistently claiming to have God on its side. Thus
in the second verse, we are reminded of the genocidal disruptions to
Native American Peoples and cultures:

Verse 2

"Oh the history books tell it
They tell it so well,
The cavalries charged
The Indians fell
The cavalries charged
The Indians died
Oh the country was young
With God on its side."

In the fourth verse, the insanity of the First World War comes
under Bob's spotlight:

Verse 4

"Oh the First World War, boys
It closed out its fate,
The reason for fighting
I never got straight;
But I learned to accept it,

Accept it with pride,
For you don't count the dead
When God's on your side."

In the seventh verse, the threat of nuclear war and the very extinction of the human race is presented as a shock-therapy, wake-up call:

Verse 7

"But now we got weapons
Of chemical dust,
If fire them we're forced to,
Then fire them we must
One push of the button
And a* shot the world wide;
And you never ask questions
When God's on your side."

a* - here I assume the first person pronoun "I" is the point of reference.

Perhaps we should all send "the Donald" a tweet message requiring him to listen to Bob's great song, again and again and again....

4.) U.S. socialist Eugene Debs had "urged workers to oppose the (First World) War, wisely observing 'Let the capitalists do their own fighting and furnish their own corpses and there will never be another war on the face of the earth'." Arrested in June 1918, and before being sentenced, having been found guilty of violating the Espionage Act, he addressed the following words to the judge:

"Your honour, years ago I recognized my kinship with all living beings, and I made up my mind that I was not one bit better than the meanest on earth. I said then and I say now, that while there is a criminal element, I am of it, while there is a soul in prison, I am not free."

SEE – <u>The Untold History Of The United States</u>. Oliver Stone and Peter Kuznick. St Ives: Ebury Press, 2012. pp xxv, 1, 5, 14-15.

<u>Who Rules The World</u>? Noam Chomsky. St Ives: Penguin Books, 2017. p7.

STRANGE TRINITY

18th January 2015

Let us bring to a long overdue conclusion
Feuds of faith, wedded to the pursuit of power,
Where anarchic hate feeds off delusion,
For those absurdly fratricidal brothers,
Mr Jew, Christian and Moslem,
Belong intrinsic to the same family,
Three muddle-headed children of Abraham,
Perversely blind to all they share in common.
So let them learn to come, often, together,
Worship under one roof, listen to each other,
Recognise, how absolutist dogma
Leads to wilful misunderstanding,
Enforces despotic dividing lines,
Desecrates sacred ground, wrecks human lives,
A state of affairs any deity
Would, I am certain, abhor and despise.

CODA: Blasphemy
The notion that
My god is better
Than yours
Thrives in millennia
Of conflict and wars.

NOTE – 1.) The former Anglican Archbishop of Capetown, anti-apartheid and human rights activist Desmond Tutu, has sagely opined:

> "To claim God exclusively for Christians is to make God too small and in a real sense is blasphemous."

2.) In 1955, five years before the end of colonial rule in Nigeria, the great educationalist Tai Solarin and his wife Sheila founded the Mayflower School, in Ikenne, situated in Ijebu Remo Division, of what was then the Western State of Nigeria. In a radical break from colonial missionary influence, "mental freedom," and a "total cleavage from all brands of religious sacerdotalism" defined the ethos of the School. "It was to belong to all, but to ride with none," a school for humanity, in a multi-faith country; and to the pupils, he made the following promise:

> "This school belongs to us. The Moslem, the Christian, the Ogun worshipper, are all equal here. This school will NEVER ask what religion a student belongs to. Our library will stock the Koran, the Bible, the Faith of Ba'Hai; books on Buddhism, on Taoism, on Confucianism. Our library will show all newspapers from anywhere in the world for you to read in your quest for knowledge."

In addition, pupils who did not wish to participate in religious services and rituals were under no pressure to do so.

SEE – Mayflower, The Story of a School. Tai Solarin. Lagos: John West Publications Ltd., 1970, pp.10-11, 52-55.

3.) Some three and a half decades ago, I recall sitting in Port Harcourt Club, Rivers State, listening, engrossed, to another Nigerian educationalist, Professor L. A. Sofenwa, describe his multi-cultural childhood, which gave him an appreciation of three religious belief systems and traditions: Yoruba, Christian and Moslem. This, he explained, came naturally, in a context where members of the same family often practised different faiths. Thus, invitations, to attend festivals and rituals, rooted in different faith traditions, helped to promote social cohesion, mutual respect and understanding. To feel at home in church and mosque, to celebrate the Yoruba gods and goddesses, the visitations of the Egungun or ancestors, Professor

Sofenwa, like Tai Solarin, recognized as expressions of an enriching, vibrant heritage.

4.) A few years ago, I became acquainted with the Rainbow Vision of the MultiFaith Chaplaincy at H.M. Prison, Canterbury. I was one of a group of visitors invited to spend a few hours in the prison and learn about the work of the chaplaincy. In Spring 2006, a new chaplaincy took shape, when the prison took on a new rôle, becoming the first international prison in the country, catering for prisoners from different countries, nationalities, cultural and religious backgrounds. As our guide, the Rev. Michael Walling explained, building on the ecumenical and multi-faith initiatives of Venerable William Noblett and the Rev. Cathy Hitchens, the new chaplaincy became a shared space, served by a team of Christian, Moslem, Jewish, Hindu, Sikh and Buddhist religious leaders, working together and, on occasion, even standing in for each other, their work characterised by respect and caritas, reaching across barriers of fear, prejudice and misunderstanding, in their efforts to meet the spiritual needs of a diverse prison population.

One prison orderly joked, that with this new system of shared space for religious observance and worship, a lot of furniture shifting and rearranging had become part of his job description. For the prisoners, shared space was both secular and religious, since they shared cells, worked and ate together. One prison officer referred to the chaplaincy team as "the conscience of the prison." By the time the prison closed seven years later, owing to budget cuts and general prison reorganization, the work of this unique MultiFaith Chaplaincy had received an R. A. Butler Trust Award for outstanding service.

MASTERS OF WAR,
VERSUS SERVANTS OF PEACE

14th August 2016

For the thirty-five devoted doctors, working
to alleviate suffering in besieged East Aleppo,
one of the most dangerous cities on earth,
including Dr Aba Zaid, Dr Hamza al Khatib,
Dr Samar Altar and Dr David Nott.

Doctors in war-ravaged East Aleppo

Freeing children, with their hands, from rubble,

Hands carrying them, gentle, tender,

Onto makeshift operating tables,

Hands performing delicate, surgical

Procedures and interventions,

Paracetamol, in lieu of anaesthetic,

Urgency, the dam restraining tears torrential,

Choices, unbearable, to be made, between

The smashed-beyond-repair

And the ones-who-might-be-saved,

While, overhead, missiles, brutal, nose-dive,

Incessant-lethal, on civilian lives,

Daily attacks on helpless humanity

Raining down, ruinous, from the bleakest skies.

After an excess of atrocities:

Chlorine gas, white phosphorous crimes,

Drone attacks and sadistic shelling,
Packaged in competing propaganda,
Or buried in conspicuous silence,
Syria's client dictator, in thrall
To a super-power proliferator
Of W.M.D., streaking unchallenged,
Across militarized skyways,
How should we deal, with a "Security Council,"
Which seems more problem than solution,
Whose members, calmly unleash
Terror, in the name of peace,
Destroying, hospitals, homes, schools,
Adding to the suffering and starvation
Of an angry, outraged population,
Trapped hostage, on besieged streets,
Waiting in vain for U.N. relief,
Demanding to know, why barbarism
Is allowed to ravage and blight their world,
And why the most powerful nations on earth,
Deal death and disservice, to those they should help?
If you care to pause and reflect for a moment,
You may well ask yourself, with rueful sigh,
Haven't we been here before, did we not
Wring our hands, with horror, to deplore
The napalm assaults on Vietnamese soil?

And that is why, those hard-pressed doctors reply;
We must speak truth to power and the world,
Whenever we have a chance, whenever time allows.
But first, we address the task in hand
To serve the Abandoned, as long as we can.

NOTE – Four out of the five permanent members of the Insecurity Council are engaged in bombing sorties over four countries in the Middle East. A nine month old baby, rushed to one of the few remaining medical centres in East Aleppo to have shrapnel extracted from his skull, knows not whether the bombs, threatening his precarious existence, come from Russian, Syrian, U.S. or other sources. That attack, one among myriads, constitutes a war crime, a flagrant violation of the Geneva Convention and those who can, must speak out, loud and clear, to the Peoples of the World, for those, whose voices are unheard, ignored or have been silenced. This obligation is part of the remit those courageous doctors have self-prescribed. They speak to stir the conscience of the World, and the daily miracles they perform in circumstances of extreme adversity, exemplify the best in humanity. They are a beacon of hope, in dark, barbaric times.

THEN AND NOW

28th September 2016

Gracias a Pablo Neruda and for
Dr David Nott and his Aleppo colleagues.

And when you ask, why doesn't her poetry

Speak of love, nature, romantic dreams

I will borrow the lines of a consummate

Wordsmith, bringing us face to face

With fascism's fury, savage-unleashed

On children, poets, flowers, markets,

Tsunamis of death on Spanish streets,

Livid-alive in Pablo's heart and mind,

Demanding utterance, public,

Through arresting poetic art,

As relevant today, as it ever was,

Explaining a few things for all of us.

Silence, unthinkable, he perceived

As self-murder, soul-suicide;

Silence would have been another form of death.

Silence would have left him, less than human,

Robbed him of that which makes life worth living.

Now, as then, for East Aleppo's doctors

And their British surgeon-teacher-brother,

Silence would have been worse than cowardice;
Silence would have been a form of death,
Handing another victory to treacherous
Generals, zealots, politician-despots
Out of control, as they perpetrate
Crimes of carnage, indiscriminate,
Against civilian-hostages
They have never seen, spoken to, or met.

Presidents Putin, Obama, Hollande, Erdoğan,
Saudi Royals and Iranian Grand Imams
And our own enigmatic-ethical,
Earnest Teresa May, or perhaps May-not,   *Theresa*
Come and see the blood in the streets,
Come and face the families bereaved.
Come and stand in the ruins of shattered
Cities, hospitals, homes, gas and water mains,
Come and see what your meddling has done,
What lies and silences cannot disguise.
Then go to Moscow and gather together,
This time, doggèd-insistent with Czar Vladimir,
Round his grand Kremlin kitchen table,
For there is vital-urgent cooking to be done;
And the results must be more than tasty,
Must satisfy the hunger
Of disunited, despairing nations.

Do not leave, until agreement is reached
And implementation seen to have started.
Do not leave, until warplanes desist
From their routine-brutal blitzkrieg,
And the Syrian-client-tyrant brought to heel.

Presidents, preachers and politicians
Listen to the silence-breakers of East Aleppo,
The exhausted doctors, indefatigable,
Unassuming heroes of the Common People,
You will never break, for they will never surrender.
Listen to the words of their brother-in-London,
The surgeon-teacher, whose support for Aleppo's
Barrel-bombed victims has never wavered.
Look into their faces, speak to them direct,
From the grandeur of your Kremlin meeting;
And stop the haemorrhage of blighted lives,
The blood in the streets, the unrelieved tears.
Listen to these doctors and follow their lead,
End the grey-crimson carnage, shown on our screens,
The shattered hearts, bitter depths of grief.
Listen to the healers, as they speak truth
To power, in the name of the People.
Listen to these doctors,
Listen to these healers,
Their concentrated wisdom

Has more to offer, is to be preferred
To the destructive arrogance
Of disconnected, deluded misleaders.
Listen to the doctors, listen to the healers.

Take from the surgeon-teacher
His proffered prescription;
Fly to Moscow, you presidents, princes,
Prime ministers, religious-political figures.
The Czar will be flattered by your coming;
And from this advantageous beginning
Ensure you go home with Peace as the prize,
This time a peace safely, securely,
Collectively negotiated,
By world leaders daring to act in unison,
Alive to the prayers of little children.
Listen to the doctors, listen to the healers;
Follow their advice, that you may heal yourselves,
And regain what you lost, in the lust for conquest.
Listen to the doctors, they are true healers;
Their love is deep, they feel for the People.
Their love flows from its source
And its source is the People.

NOTE – Pablo Neruda (1904-1973) is regarded as one of the key
poetic figures of the twentieth century. In his poem "Explico Algu-
nas Cosas" (I'm Explaining a Few Things), Pablo Neruda's "sense

of personal outrage" at the destructive horrors of the Spanish Civil War, "flows into a political confrontation." The poetic discourse is both public and personal, poetry as "a form of utterance." Jean Franco argues "we cannot take Neruda's poetry without the political nettle, without the vision of unalienated man, of justice and equality on earth," and so, in his rôle as public poet, he "address(es) himself to a community, not simply as an individual, but as their voice."

Through their medical work and public utterances on the war, or rather wars, raging in Syria, the doctors of East Aleppo speak, on behalf of and for the communities they serve.

Pablo Neruda makes us see, feel and react to the crimes perpetrated by Franco's generals. A dialogue, in the form of question and answer, is used to challenge the listener:

Treacherous
generals:
see my dead house
look at broken Spain:
from every house burning metal flows
instead of flowers,
from every socket of Spain
Spain emerges
and from every dead child a rifle with eyes,
and from every crime bullets are born
which will one day find
the bull's eye of your hearts.

And you will ask: why doesn't his poetry
speak of dreams and leaves
and the great volcanoes of his native land?

Come and see the blood in the streets.
Come and see
the blood in the streets
Come and see the blood
in the streets!

SEE – <u>Pablo Neruda. Selected Poems</u>. A bi-lingual edition. edited by Nathaniel Tarn. Harmondsworth: Penguin Book Ltd., 1979, p.13, 17 and pp.103-107.

VARIATIONS ON EXISTENTIAL QUESTIONS

5th February 2017

OF WEALTH AND POVERTY

Number One

for John Cairney and in honour of his parents
Mary and Tom.
Place – Glasgow, Year – 1962

Wee lass, ignorant-cocooned in fragile

False-privileged segregation,

Garden-fenced in middle-class

Precarious, suburban isolation,

How could you see beyond the Gorbals'[1.]

Glowering, grim-forbidding exteriors?

How could you know the strength and love

Holding families and neighbours thegither,

Tighter than any unkin' stramash

Of cronies, unco fu'[2.] on a Saturday nicht,

Men whose skills, ingenuity, labour

Built the second city of a cruel empire,

Welders, plumbers, carpenters, electricians

Builders, drivers, refuse collectors, mechanics,

Their wives manufacturing civilization,
Tender comfort, solidarity, loyalty,
From the meagre resources at their disposal,
Each day working miracles, quintessential,
Unremarked, unrecorded, taken for granted.

When word raced with greyhound streaking speed,
Along winding alleys, across dark, dreary closes,
Up-an-doun the stairs o' cramped hamely spaces,
The gaunt tenements housing poor-rich families,
Mary's neighbours, friends, casual acquaintances
Soon heard of her frustrated remonstrations,
Articulated, clarion-clear-uninhibited,
On Effie Reid's phone, affixed helpful
To the shop wall, where it served the community
In mair ways than wan, as Effie listened intent,
Then serviced her network of gossip-guzzling friends.
"I canna go, son, I've naething to wear."
Her son, for his part, was quick to retort
"But you must, it's a Royal Command Performance.
You can't disappoint both your actor-son
And visiting Majesties, frae London and Stockholm!"
"I've tauld you wance, must I tell you again;
I canna compete with tiaras and gowns,
I've naething to wear, amang sich a posh crowd."
John's riposte tripped cheeky-daft, aff his tongue,

"Then go as a nudist, but please just come.
It should be a special, joyful occasion,
In any event, just you remember
Oor ain folk are every bit as good as their lot,
Come tae think of it, a guid deal better!"
Mary went home, despondent, downcast,
Meanwhile Effie took the matter in hand,
Spreading the word to the public at large.
Soon John's Dad remarked to his Wife
"I've never known sich an influx o' visitors
Bringing sae many claes[3.] fer you to choose frae."
Gloves, shoes in assorted styles and colours,
A silk scarf, fox fur, dress-coat in barathea,
A string of pearls, top-quality imitation,
Were laid, in loving profusion before her,
By women, determined to play their part
And bridge the stand-off between Mither-an'-Son.
Now happiness shone in Mary's eyes and smile,
"I feel like a Glasgie wifie-an-mither[4.]
Turned, for a while, into a lucky Cinderella
Made ready for a very splendid occasion,
By the combined magic of Glaswegian
Phenomenal fairy Godmithers,
From part of oor city some label and call
A dangerous, dirt-poor cesspit of violence,

Yet who in their richt mind would want

Tae live in lonely-formal palatial splendour,

Far frae ordinary folk, wi' no airs or graces,

Folk, whae come to your aid, wi' oot yer asking them,

Folk, whae hae[5] jus' brought quarrelling

Mither-an'-Son back thegither again,

Folk, whase kindness gies life richer meaning."

John's Dad poured a wee dram[6] in celebration.

"I agree with your overall assessment;

But dinna forget oor families an' friends

Deserve mair respect from the City Faethers,

Industrialists, stockbrokers and bankers

Now dinna get me wrang, I wouldna wan'

Tae live in Milngavie or Kelvinside[7];

But hae we no, lang sin' earned the recht

Tae better, brighter accommodation,

Decent-sized rooms, in council houses

Wi' gardens fit for the weans[8] tae play in

Whit I'm asking fer, my precious woman,

Is whit I wid want for every citizen,

The longed-for accession tae true civilization,

Whar there's a place fir everywan at the table,

Folk from the Gorbals, hob-nobbing wi' royalty

But wi' none o' that slavish kow-towing,

In shamefaced, fawning servility

And in the spirit o' Rabbie Burns'

Stubborn, egalitarian insistence,

I can see nae guid reason, whitsoever

Tae maintain unhealthy social divisions,

Perpetuating hurt and harm tae oor nation.

But richt noo, my bonnie lass, it's aff

Tae Auld Reekie[9.], John an' the Lyceum,

Alang wi' your needfu'[10.] finery,

Tae celebrate oor son's achievement."

NOTE – 1.) John Cairney's description of a very special 1962 Royal Command Performance has stayed with me for many years. It is the source of inspiration for this poem, which leads into the second of the sequence, although "In My End Is My Beginning" was written four months earlier and starts with the impact of those louring tenement façades, on my childhood imagination. Hence, on offer are contrasting social perspectives, at variance, in collision, yet at the same time, linked in their jarring dissonance.

SEE – East End To West End, First Steps in an Autobiographical Journey. John Cairney. Edinburgh: Mainstream Publishing Company Ltd., 1988, pp.208-212.

2.) The following lines honour the unrecorded heroism of Scottish working class women and the insensitivity of many men to the price their wives, mothers and sisters all too often paid, and for that matter continue to pay:

> "With a few pounds and some sticks of furniture, they had every day practised a very commonplace white magic. They had sewn comfort out of rags, brewed surprising satisfaction from unimpressive ingredients, calmed storms and taught decency in the face of the injustice their own lives suffered. But the cost of it had often been themselves. They were the ingredients of their own magic, last ounce of spirit, last shred of ambition,

smallest fragment of dream. The wastage - the good minds starved, the talents denied, the potential distorted - was beyond computation."

In this passage, a sober, reflective Dan Scoular, the central character of the novel, is taking stock of the rôles played by his own Wife and Mother in their families and communities. His thoughts begin to extend beyond the purely personal to the public, the political, to the countless, unrecognized, un- or underappreciated heroic women like them, women whose efforts and unstated self-sacrifice are simply taken for granted by their menfolk. At this juncture, Dan, having only recently discovered the harsh reality of his own Mother's struggle against poverty, throughout his childhood and youth, recognizes that he too has taken so much, indeed far too much for granted. A new state of consciousness emerges triggering shame and regret, and importantly the understanding that such heroism "was a dubious commodity":

> "That lost army of fraught, unglamorous women with the coats they had to make last for years and the shoes inside which strips of cardboard, absorbing dampness, recorded the passage of hard times like the rings of a dead tree, had done unbelievable things. But they shouldn't have been asked to do them."

The late William McIlvanney's magnificent poetic-prose, his holistic understanding of how society functions and malfunctions, his commitment to social justice and truth-telling have also inspired "Of Wealth And Poverty" and indeed the poem which follows.

SEE – The Big Man. William McIlvanney. London: Hodder and Stoughton, 1985, p.148.

3.) In the following glossary of Scots words used in "Of Wealth And Poverty," I decided to include only those words which readers and listeners might find difficult to understand:

the Gorbals[1.] -a working class district of Glasgow, on the south bank of the River Clyde, notable in the past for its overcrowded tenements and traditions of working class solidarity, also famous for its great cultural treasure, The Citizens' Theatre, established to make great theatre, international, as well as national and regional, accessible to all, at prices modest and affordable. The overcrowded tenements have gone. The theatre, founded on democratic principles, survives and thrives.

unkin' stramash / Of cronies unco fu'[2.] -a temporary falling out of friends, who have imbibed too much alcohol, leading to a brawl.

claes[3.] -clothes.

a Glasgie wifie-an-mither[4.] -a Glaswegian wife and mother (Glaswegian, meaning from or belonging to Glasgow).

whae hae[5.] -who have.

a wee dram[6.] -a small draught/measurement of spirits, especially whisky.

Milngavie or Kelvinside[7.] -two middle-class areas of Glasgow and environs: Milngavie, a prosperous suburb at the northwestern edge of Greater Glasgow, Kelvinside nearer the centre.

weans[8.] -children

Auld Reekie[9.] -an epithet for Edinburgh meaning Old and Smoky, hardly flattering, but, strange to tell, conveying derisive affection. The reference is, of course, to air pollution, especially with regard to the period when coal was the principal source of energy.

needfu'[10.] -necessary, essential.

IN MY END IS MY BEGINNING

30th September 2016

Number Two

Glasgow and Paisley 1952, Canterbury 2016

Wee lass, pigtails looped, glossy beribboned,
I see you snug-nestled under tartan rug,
Sleepy-dreamy on dark green leather seat,
Behind Father at the wheel, Mother sitting
Elegant at his side, surface-contented,
A teacher, exiled in nineteen fifties,
Bourgeois-mandated domestic diligence,
A wife, a mother, home-maker meticulous,
A conscientious-tense, quiet conformist,
Hungry for what she had achieved, then lost,
Cigarette glamour, exhaled in style
Emanating slow from her ruby lips,
As Father chuckling-genial, shakes his head.
You must be the only Sassenach[1.] wife in town,
Reluctant to yield to your husband's fond wish
To buy you a new suit or cocktail gown,
From one of Glasgow's most fashionable shops.
How often had I heard Mother remonstrate,
But I have no need of a new winter suit,

And the gown you like is so overpriced;
In any case, they don't have my size.
Och lass, what is a man to do, faced
With your puritanical self-denial?
But, do you really have the right to deny me
The pleasure of expressing appreciation
For your homemaking skills and devotion?
Then laughter would follow, as my Father,
Triumphant, would add, when you were in the Ladies'
Powdering your nose, I took the liberty
Of ordering that dress, it should be with you,
By post, next week, in time for the works'
Dinner-dance at the Brabloch hotel,
Now not another word, for the deed is done!
My Mother would first frown, then shake her head,
Throw up her hands in mock resignation,
Then kiss the man she loved, fretted over,
My Father laughing-bemused, my Mother smiling,
Her eyes deep-blue, mischievous-twinkling.

The bright lights of toy shops, restaurants,
Palatial emporia, stocked with temptation,
Would give way to the grey of darkening skies,
As we skirted the Gorbals[2], and day turned to night.
Wee lass, I see you, puzzled, perplexed
By the unexplained, clashing contrasts, glimpsed

From the tartan-rug-warmth of that car-in-motion,
Peeping through the window, at bleak tombstone
Tenement buildings, formidable-fearsome,
Prison-like-grim, scowling and sullen.
How many children, you asked yourself,
Lived buried inside those dismal spaces,
Denied, cut off from the good things of life,
Like the Little Matchgirl, hungry, alone,
A Cinderella, forlorn, without her Prince,
Trapped in a cruel, indifferent world?
In my childish head, on those journeys home,
Questions, confusing, began to form,
Subversive-dormant, haunting, unspoken,
Because intuition told me, warned me
They would not be welcomed, by parents
Enjoying a little privileged escapism,
In a bustling, commercial-industrial centre,
The second city of a moribund empire.
In bed at night, cosy-snug and well-fed,
I thought of the honeysuckle, climbing
The pipe in early summer profusion,
Outside my bedroom, its perfumed fragrance,
A kiss from nature, the chirruping sounds
From the nest, cradled in that floral bower,
A sign that all was well in my Arkleston

Bungalow home; but why I wondered, wanted to know,
Did some children live in gloomy-grey spaces,
While I had strawberries, verdant lawns and flowers;
And why hadn't God, and Jesus his Son
Who loved little children, arranged things better?
I wanted to ask my Sunday school teacher
Why Jesus seemed to have forgotten the Gorbals?
Why did I enjoy so much, while they remained
Starved of beauty, left in the lurch?
But I knew in Paisley Abbey, my words
Would not be welcomed, so bewildered,
I buttoned my lips and kept them hidden.

Now in the twilight years of mortal existence,
The same questions, secular-reworded,
Echoing Kwame Nkrumah's injunction:
Seek ye first the political kingdom,
Still storm my senses, demand attention,
As I see starvation, rampant malnutrition
Etched intolerable, on the young-old
Faces of children and babes in their millions,
Their Mothers' breasts, devoid of nourishment,
In countries where our drones and military
Off-load bombs in the name of liberty,
While government ministers proudly proclaim
Britain is the sixth richest country in the world,

And arms manufacturers amass hidden fortunes.
The wee lass, nestling under tartan rug,
Now a woman of seventy, spurred to anger,
Still demands answers to the same urgent questions.
Today, our rich-poor Disunited Queendom,
Spawns a proliferation of under-reported
Soup kitchens, food banks and breakfast clubs
For hungry, unhappy British children,
A new generation of Oliver Twists
Born into the disequilibrium
Of an ugly-cruel, regressive era.
Is this not a shameful state of affairs,
In a country whose leaders proclaim its wealth?
This woman of seventy is still the girl of seven
Instinctively questioning, the sensed
Injustice, of children sentenced from birth
To callous indifference, exploitation or worse.
In our shrouded past, as in our present,
Empires futile, rise and fall,
Unstable pyramids of discontent,
Justice denied, slavery entrenched.
Why then do we remain blind to the harm
That we do, the harm we have done?
Why are deluded warring factions,
Regions, nations, trans-continental corporations

Wedded to systems of sustained misery?
Why do we not build better futures,
Better living conditions, for the Common People,
Decent houses with gardens, near well-tended parks,
So that nature and human-made infrastructure
Work together, integrated in harmony,
And living in this green and pleasant land,
Children no longer denied their birthright?
And beyond our island homes, let there be
No more uprooted child-refugees,
Dying abandoned on land, or drowning at sea,
No more children, trafficked into sex-slavery,
No more child-soldiers, moulded into killers,
No more girls, gang-raped by zealots deranged,
No more girls, deprived of an education,
Sentenced to unpaid domestic labour,
Vulnerable-ripe for sexploitation,
No more seventy-year-old angry women,
Still demanding answers to old-urgent questions
First formed in lonely, puzzled childhood silence:
How to share the Earth we all inhabit?
How to evolve beyond doomed imperial habits?

In my end is my beginning
The dreams I cherish, undiminished,
They are expressions of love's power

And in my soul, still blossom and flower,
For love is life; without love we die,
Self-exiled, lonely, in arid deserts,
Denying ourselves our very humanity.
In loving Earth, friends, neighbours, family
We increase our capacity for empathy,
Growing beyond reductive obsessions,
Reaching across angry borders and boundaries
To reclaim our common humanity.
Just as hate diminishes, love enhances
The capacity to feel the pain of others,
Pushing down barricades, extending horizons.
In my end is my beginning,
The dreams I cherish undiminished.
Let them find homes in hungry hearts
For they belong to each and every one of us.

NOTE – Sassenach[1] -the name given by the Gaelic inhabitants of Britain and Ireland to their "Saxon" or English neighbours.
the Gorbals[2] -SEE Of Wealth And Poverty, the Glossary section, first reference, pp 293-294.